THE CITIZENS ACADEMY HANDBOOK

Building Capacity for Local Civic Engagement

Ricardo S. Morse

Sabrina M. Willard

Michelle Y. Holder

UNC
SCHOOL OF GOVERNMENT

The School of Government at the University of North Carolina at Chapel Hill works to improve the lives of North Carolinians by engaging in practical scholarship that helps public officials and citizens understand and improve state and local government. Established in 1931 as the Institute of Government, the School provides educational, advisory, and research services for state and local governments. The School of Government is also home to a nationally ranked Master of Public Administration program, the North Carolina Judicial College, and specialized centers focused on community and economic development, information technology, and environmental finance.

As the largest university-based local government training, advisory, and research organization in the United States, the School of Government offers up to 200 courses, webinars, and specialized conferences for more than 12,000 public officials each year. In addition, faculty members annually publish approximately 50 books, manuals, reports, articles, bulletins, and other print and online content related to state and local government. The School also produces the *Daily Bulletin Online* each day the General Assembly is in session, reporting on activities for members of the legislature and others who need to follow the course of legislation.

Operating support for the School of Government's programs and activities comes from many sources, including state appropriations, local government membership dues, private contributions, publication sales, course fees, and service contracts.

Michael R. Smith, Dean
Thomas H. Thornburg, Senior Associate Dean
Frayda S. Bluestein, Associate Dean for Faculty Development
Johnny Burleson, Associate Dean for Development
Michael Vollmer, Associate Dean for Administration
Linda H. Weiner, Associate Dean for Operations
Janet Holston, Director of Strategy and Innovation

FACULTY

Whitney Afonso	James C. Drennan	Christopher B. McLaughlin	Jessica Smith
Trey Allen	Richard D. Ducker	Kara A. Millonzi	Meredith Smith
Gregory S. Allison	Robert L. Farb	Jill D. Moore	Carl W. Stenberg III
David N. Ammons	Norma Houston	Jonathan Q. Morgan	John B. Stephens
Ann M. Anderson	Cheryl Daniels Howell	Ricardo S. Morse	Charles Szypszak
Maureen Berner	Jeffrey A. Hughes	C. Tyler Mulligan	Shannon H. Tufts
Mark F. Botts	Willow S. Jacobson	Kimberly L. Nelson	Vaughn Mamlin Upshaw
Anita R. Brown-Graham	Robert P. Joyce	David W. Owens	Aimee N. Wall
Peg Carlson	Diane M. Juffras	LaToya B. Powell	Jeffrey B. Welty
Leisha DeHart-Davis	Dona G. Lewandowski	William C. Rivenbark	Richard B. Whisnant
Shea Riggsbee Denning	Adam Lovelady	Dale J. Roenigk	
Sara DePasquale	James M. Markham	John Rubin	

Contents

Preface

Engaging citizens in local governance is not a fad or simply a nice thing to do. It is, rather, at the core of self-governance. Because local government is closest to the people, it provides the greatest opportunity for citizens to meaningfully participate in the governance process beyond merely voting.

Thus the question for local government leaders in the twenty-first century is not *whether* they should engage citizens, but *how*. How can citizens be meaningfully and productively engaged in local governance? How can engagement add value both to the local government and to the citizens they serve? How can positive engagement be cultivated when people are so busy and when knowledge about local governance is generally low?

Citizens academies are one way for local governments to address the question of "how?" Citizens academies are being used to till the gardens of democracy that are our local communities, to plant seeds that, with proper tending, put forth shoots that grow into greater and better citizen engagement, community leadership, and goodwill between citizens and local officials. This is not to say that citizens academies are a cure-all for the difficulties inherent in citizen and community engagement, but certainly they are a low-cost, high-return opportunity to make a difference.

This handbook is offered as an introduction to the practice of citizens (or local government) academies as an innovative approach to civic education and capacity building. It is provided also as a resource for local government officials or other individuals or groups who are already conducting citizens academies or are contemplating doing so. These pages provide guidance on all aspects of program planning and execution. Whether for a program that has been going for years or is in the process of being developed, concrete, hands-on information can be found here.

As both an introduction to the topic and a nuts and bolts handbook, this guide is intended for a broad audience. We believe it should be of particular interest to local elected officials, managers/administrators, public information and community relations officers, and others in local government who are interested in developing citizen engagement. It should also be of interest to other civic-oriented organizations that partner with, or might partner with, local governments to conduct a citizens academy. Finally, this handbook will be most useful to those who actually run citizens academies by providing how-to advice as well as offering insights and ideas that could help existing programs go from *good* to *great*.

Like many public-minded projects, this one would not have been possible without help, in this case from dozens of program coordinators who over the past few years have graciously shared with us their experiences, program materials, and group pictures. We thank each of them for taking the time to help us with this project and for their enthusiasm for civic engagement.

For financial support, we want to thank the North Carolina City County Manager's Association and the UNC School of Government. Thanks are due also to John Stephens, Peter Franzese, and Jennifer Della Valle, who reviewed an early draft and provided valuable feedback. We also wish to thank the publications team at the School of Government, who have been tremendously helpful throughout this process.

Finally, a special debt of gratitude is owed to Seth Cutter, a graduate of the Master of Public Administration program at the School of Government who worked with Rick in 2011–2012 researching citizens academies, building a database of programs, constructing a resource website, and helping lay the foundation for this handbook. Without Seth's work, this project would never have gotten off the ground.

Also, we want to emphasize that this handbook is part of a larger project to provide resources and capacity building for organizations that offer citizens academies or are considering doing so. Our goal is to build a community of practice around citizens academies, and we plan to continue developing the citizens academies website as a means of facilitating that effort. Located at www.sog.unc.edu/resources/microsites/citizens-academies, the website is a repository of additional resources that augment what is presented in these pages: case studies, links to research and other relevant resources, and a database of programs (as well as a link to a form for updating program information in the database). We welcome suggestions on how to maximize the website as a resource to accompany this handbook.

We are particularly interested in hearing more stories about how citizens academies are run and the innovative approaches that various local governments are employing to maximize their potential in terms of building civic capacity. We anticipate updating this book in the future and would like to know what information contained herein is most useful to readers as well as what additional information and tools would be useful. Please send suggestions for a future edition of this book or for adding resources to the website, and/or information on innovative practices and success stories, to Rick Morse at rmorse@sog.unc.edu.

We hope you will find in this handbook both inspiration and assistance in your efforts to nurture more positive and efficacious civic engagement within your communities. We also hope you will connect with us online via the website to help continue to develop the citizens academy knowledge base.

Ricardo S. Morse
Sabrina M. Willard
Michelle Y. Holder

January 2017

1. Building Capacity for Civic Engagement

> *Attending the Town of Cary School of Government increased my awareness about how towns function and how this Town—both politicians and staff—have pressed for positive growth, operational excellence, and community participation. The experience of learning and meeting staff members and seeing firsthand how our Town operates made me more appreciative, more interested, more invested, and— ultimately—more involved and supportive.*
>
> 2010 Graduate of the Cary, North Carolina, School of Government

Civic engagement is at the forefront of contemporary thinking and local government practice.[1] Consider the following statement from the National League of Cities (NLC):

> NLC is contributing to a national effort to strengthen democracy and governance at the local level by involving residents in government and public life and by focusing on developing an inclusive, collaborative, and effective relationship built on trust between citizens

---

1. This chapter is derived, in part, from Ricardo S. Morse, "Citizens Academies: Local Governments Building Capacity for Citizen Engagement," *Public Performance & Management Review* 36, no. 1 (2012): 79–101, www.tandfonline.com/doi/abs/10.2753/PMR1530-9576360104.

and government. Through these relationships, communities can work together to arrive at solutions to pressing problems.[2]

The International City/County Management Association (ICMA) is similarly focused on civic engagement. Its Center for Management Strategies has identified civic engagement as a "leading practice":

> Engaging the public in local decision making and community building is critically important work for any local government. . . . Engaging residents and other stakeholders can increase understanding, create better and more sustainable decisions, and build trust. It can also build better, more cohesive communities and improve customer satisfaction.[3]

Public administration scholars, and scholars of local government in particular, have for some time highlighted the importance of civic engagement as a key feature of good governance. An extensive review of the topic written by prominent public administration scholars Jim Svara and Janet Denhardt observes that "many local governments are examining ways to increase the opportunities for residents to be engaged in informed discussion with each other and with government officials."[4] Svara and Denhardt find two primary reasons for this increased emphasis on engagement: it is the "right" as well as the "smart" thing to do. It is the "right" thing inasmuch as it reflects widespread values associated with democratic self-governance and community.[5] It is the "smart" thing in that "effective governance at the local level increasingly requires active and ongoing citizen participation"

---

2. From the Civic Engagement resource page on the National League of Cities website, www.nlc.org/find-city-solutions/city-solutions-and-applied-research/governance/civic-engagement (last accessed Aug. 5, 2016).

3. See the Civic Engagement page of the ICMA website at icma.org/en/results/management_strategies/leading_practices/civic_engagement (last accessed Aug. 5, 2016).

4. James H. Svara and Janet V. Denhardt, eds., "Connected Communities: Local Governments as a Partner in Citizen Engagement and Community Building," white paper (Phoenix, Ariz.: ICMA Alliance for Innovation, Oct. 15, 2010), 7, http://icma.org/en/icma/knowledge_network/documents/kn/document/301763/connected_communities_local_governments_as_a_partner_in_citizen_engagement_and_community_building.

5. Svara and Denhardt, "Connected Communities," 6–7.

because "the complexity of the problems facing local government demands citizen involvement and acceptance, if not cooperation."[6]

The increasing emphasis on civic engagement points to the underlying issue of *how communities can build capacity for collaboration and engagement.* Local government leaders may have a strong *commitment* to civic engagement, but, ultimately, success is dependent on the *capability* and *willingness* of citizens, groups, and organizations within the community to become engaged as effective partners in local governance. The development of citizens academies in communities across the United States is an innovative practice that represents direct efforts by local governments to build such capacity for civic engagement.

This handbook offers practical advice for individuals and groups that coordinate citizens academies or are in the process of creating a citizens academy. It offers nuts-and-bolts advice on all aspects of program planning and delivery and is meant to be a helpful starting point for organizations that are starting new programs or contemplating creating a citizens academy. It also highlights many ideas and innovations that should be useful to even the most well-established programs. But before delving into those programmatic details, it is important to first clarify the *what* and the *why* of citizens academies.

Local Government Efforts on Behalf of Civic Engagement

As noted above, the rise of citizens academies occurs within a context of greater interest in, and appreciation of, civic engagement in local government practice. The term (citizen, civic, public, or community) *engagement* is used purposively here to reflect a more substantive approach to what has long been referred to as "citizen participation" in local government. Carolyn Lukensmeyer and Lars Torres explain that "engagement" refers to "forums that bring the general, impacted public into partnership with decision makers through dialogue-based processes at points along the policy-development continuum."[7] Svara and Denhardt note that "citizen engagement focuses on revitalizing democracy, building citizenship

---

6. Svara and Denhardt, "Connected Communities," 7.

7. Carolyn J. Lukensmeyer and Lars Hasselblad Torres, *Public Deliberation: A Manager's Guide to Citizen Engagement* (Washington, D.C.: IBM center for the Business of Government, 2006), 9.

2015 Participants in the Clearwater (Fla.) 101 Program (Photo courtesy of the City of Clearwater)

and reinforcing a sense of community, and it cannot be equated with one-way exchanges between government and citizens."[8]

Also noted above, this emphasis on civic engagement is at the forefront of local government practice. A 2009 NLC survey of municipal elected officials found that 81 percent of respondents reported that their municipalities use "public engagement processes" often or sometimes.[9] Also, 85 percent of respondents reported that they participate in public engagement more than is required by law. In addition, 67 percent reported regularly using "special deliberative processes," whereas 95 percent answered that they value public engagement "to a great extent" (58%) or at least "somewhat" (37%).

While local public officials are generally supportive of citizen engagement, questions remain as to the capacity of community stakeholders to become successfully

---

8. Svara and Denhardt, "Connected Communities," 4.

9. William Barnes and Bonnie C. Mann, "Making Local Democracy Work: Municipal Officials' Views about Public Engagement." *National Civic Review* 100, no. 3 (2011): 58–62.

engaged as partners in governance. A 2010 study of America's civic health, sponsored by the Corporation for National and Community Service and the National Conference on Citizenship, found that only *9 percent* of respondents had attended a public meeting in the past two years.[10] The prevalent view of citizen involvement efforts in local government, according to a 2007 study, is that both citizens and administrators are often too busy for "meaningful citizen participation in the governing process."[11] Generalized citizen discontent also continues to be a problem, at all levels of government, particularly in the aftermath of the great recession of 2008–2009.[12]

Carmen Sirianni makes a strong argument in his excellent book *Investing in Democracy* that the "costs of self-governance" are rising. Increasingly, complex public problems, a "growing diversity of publics," and (somewhat ironically) "rising public expectations for voice and inclusion" have created a situation in great need of "enhanced civic skill sets and organizational capacities."[13] While recognizing the important work of the civic or nongovernmental sector in the work of civic or community capacity building, Sirianni reminds us that the public sector "has a fundamental and fully legitimate interest in its citizens having the requisite civic skills, networks, and deliberative forums needed to sustain a self-governing republic."[14] He therefore argues for *purposeful investments by governments* in "civic capacity building" which ensure that their "partners have capacities for fair and informed deliberation and shared work."[15]

The National Civic League (NCL) has over many decades been a strong advocate of the development of civic capacity in local communities. The "civic index" is a set of indicators developed by the NCL to try and capture or measure a community's "civic infrastructure," defined as "formal and informal processes and networks

---

10. Corporation for National and Community Service (CNCS) and the National Conference on Citizenship (NCoC), *Civic Life in America: Key Findings on the Civic Health of the Nation*, issue brief (Washington, D.C.: CNCS and NCoC, September 2010).

11. Kaifeng Yang and Kathe Callahan, "Citizen Involvement Efforts and Bureaucratic Responsiveness: Participatory Values, Stakeholder Pressures, and Administrative Practicality." *Public Administration Review* 67, no. 2 (2007): 249–64.

12. Cheryl Simrell King and Renee Nank, "Citizens, Administrators, and Their Discontents," in *Government Is Us 2.0*, edited by Cheryl Simrell King (Armonk, N.Y.: M. E. Sharpe, 2011), 3–16.

13. Carmen Sirianni, *Investing in Democracy: Engaging Citizens in Collaborative Governance* (Washington, D.C.: Brookings Institution Press, 2009), 13–18.

14. Sirianni, *Investing in Democracy*, 20.

15. Sirianni, *Investing in Democracy*, 21.

through which communities make decisions and attempt to solve problems."[16] One of the indicators is the extent to which communities have means to "teach citizens how to be effective community members."[17]

Community networks and structured mechanisms for engagement can work only if the individuals involved have the basic competencies needed to meaningfully participate. Public administration scholars Kathe Callahan and Kaifeng Yang argue that "in order to contribute in a meaningful way, citizens need to be informed about the issues and understand how government functions."[18] William Galston of the Brookings Institution similarly concludes that "recent research shows that if we want to revitalize and sustain democratic citizenship, working to raise levels of civic knowledge and information would be one effective strategy, and a sensible place to begin."[19]

Callahan and Yang point out that effective engagement and collaboration can work only if and when citizens have "the time and the interest," which itself is dependent on them understanding "the functions of government so they are aware of opportunities, as well as constraints."[20] Citing lack of expertise as a common barrier to meaningful participation, these scholars also suggest that "administrators may proactively respond to some participation barriers by providing more participation opportunities and support."[21] One of their key conclusions is that "*training and education for citizens* and administrators is essential if the public sector is to experience meaningful civic

> *... if we want to revitalize and sustain democratic citizenship, working to raise levels of civic knowledge and information would be one effective strategy, and a sensible place to begin.*
>
> William Galston,
> Brookings Institution

16. Derek Okubo, Christopher T. Gates, and Gloria Rubio-Cortes, "Questions to Ask: Components of the Civic Index." *National Civic Review* 88, no. 4 (1999): 271–92; quote at 271.

17. Okubo, Gates, and Rubio-Cortes, "Questions to Ask," 286.

18. Kathe Callahan and Kaifeng Yang, "Training and Professional Development for Civically Engaged Communities." *Innovation Journal* 10, no. 1 (2005): 1–16; quote at 1.

19. William A. Galston, "Civic Knowledge, Civic Education, and Civic Engagement: A Summary of Recent Research." *International Journal of Public Administration* 30, nos. 6–7 (2007): 623–42; quote at 624.

20. Callahan and Yang, "Training and Professional Development for Civically Engaged Communities," 4.

21. Kaifeng Yang and Kathe Callahan, "Citizen Involvement Efforts and Bureaucratic Responsiveness: Participatory Values, Stakeholder Pressures, and Administrative Practicality." *Public Administration Review* 67, no. 2 (2007): 249–64; quote at 260.

participation."[22] This conclusion echoes a recommendation by Cheryl King, Kathryn Feltey, and Bridget Susel in their seminal article on "authentic participation" that public administrators "teach citizens how to work within the system and to work with the system."[23]

The idea that citizens (and public officials) need to be educated in order to build capacity for local civic engagement is supported by numerous studies which "demonstrate that civic knowledge is an important determinant of civic capability and character."[24] The 2009 NLC survey of municipal officials mentioned above finds close to half of all respondents saying that citizens lack the "necessary skills and knowledge to [engage] effectively" and that they "need more training for engagement processes."[25] Citizens academies are one such way of developing educational opportunities aimed at building civic competence among the local citizenry.[26]

> *In order to contribute in a meaningful way, citizens need to be informed about the issues and understand how government functions.*
>
> Kathe Callahan and Kaifeng Yang

Citizens Academies

Citizens academies are educational programs conducted by cities and counties for the purpose of better informing and engaging citizens. Citizens academies are a relatively recent but growing phenomenon in the United States. A few early programs appeared in the late 1990s, but the vast majority were created in the 2000s, and new ones kick off each year.

There is some question as to whether the proper term should be *citizens, citizen's, citizens',* or *citizen* academies. We use *citizens* here because it is the variation most commonly used among the dozens of such programs we have examined.

---

22. Callahan and Yang, "Training and Professional Development for Civically Engaged Communities," 4 (emphasis added).

23. Cheryl Simrell King, Kathryn M. Feltey, and Bridget O'Neill Susel, "The Question of Participation: Toward Authentic Public Participation in Public Administration." *Public Administration Review* 58, no. 4 (1998): 317–26; quote at 324.

24. Galston, "Civic Knowledge, Civic Education, and Civic Engagement," 639.

25. William Barnes and Bonnie C. Mann, *Making Local Democracy Work: Municipal Officials' Views about Public Engagement.* Research Report. Washington, D.C.: National League of Cities Center for Research and Innovation, 2010; quotes at 21 and iii.

26. Callahan and Yang, "Training and Professional Development for Civically Engaged Communities," 11.

> *Citizens academies seems to be the most common term for these programs. Other names that these programs commonly go by include local government academies, city or county academies, neighborhood colleges, and city or county 101.*

The absence of an apostrophe helps avoid the implication that programs are owned or controlled by citizens groups. *Citizen* might be problematic in that it could suggest that the program is about how one becomes a citizen. *Citizens*, on the other hand, appropriately implies that a program is *for* citizens (or, more properly, residents) of a local community. The term may be advantageous also in emphasizing the ideal of citizenship in terms of being a responsible citizen, having a sense of civic duty, and so on.

On the other hand, the term *citizen* in the title of a program could appear to be exclusive, that is, imply that one must be a *legal* citizen to participate. Thus there are many other names these programs go by, the most common being local government academies, city or county academies, neighborhood colleges, city or county 101, city or county university, and city or county school of government. Certainly the name of the program should be inclusive and make sense in terms of the local culture. Our use of the term *citizens* is merely for simplicity's sake and is not meant to imply that it is the most appropriate name for these programs.

Related or Similar Programs
Citizens academies are related to, or could be viewed as offshoots of, two other types of community-based civic education programs, citizen police academies (CPAs) and community leadership programs (CLPs). CPAs—and their similar, though less common cousins, citizen fire academies and citizen planning academies—are programs sponsored by specific divisions of local government aimed at informing citizens about the work of that particular division.

CPAs are very common throughout the United States, with "as many as 45 percent of police departments offer[ing] some form of a citizen police academy." In fact, the majority of hits that result from Googling "citizens academies" link to actual CPAs or to other public safety academies. Not only do CPAs provide opportunities for informing citizens of police operations, but they also enable positive citizen-officer interactions and "develop a relationship of trust and cooperation between the police and citizens."[27] CPAs seem to be the direct antecedent of citizens academies because they have been around for a longer period of time, are more widespread, and generally are quite popular. The Federal Bureau of Investigation even runs citizens academies out of its field offices.[28] But the purposes of citizens *police* academies are fairly narrow and should not be viewed as meeting the broader goals of the type of program described in this handbook.

Community leadership programs, or CLPs, also seem to have been an inspiration for citizens academies and, like CPAs, are widespread throughout the United States. According to a 2010 report, CLPs exist "in thousands of large and small cities and communities across the United States (and more recently internationally) . . . for the purpose of developing active and informed citizen leaders who can collaborate with other individuals and groups to solve community-based problems."[29] These programs are sponsored most often by the local chamber of commerce but also sometimes by the United Way or other non-profit organization.[30]

Citizens academies are similar to CPAs and CLPs but also are different in important ways. Like CPAs, citizens academies provide civic education programs for local citizens conducted by local government. CLPs are similar to citizens academies in that they cover a broad range of topics and seek to develop civic capacity through civic education.

Unlike citizens academies, CPAs are conducted by a single division of government (law enforcement) and focus solely on that function (as opposed to the enterprise-wide emphasis of citizens academies). CLPs differ from citizens academies in that they are sponsored—and, for the most part, conducted—by non-governmental organizations. Also, even though some program content is likely to be about local government, CLPs typically have a broader curriculum than that of citizens academies because they emphasize civic leadership skills as much as civic knowledge, whereas citizens academies are mostly about developing civic

---

27. J. Bret Becton, Leslie Meadows, Rachel Tears, Michael Charles, and Ralph Ioimo, "Can Citizen Police Academies Influence Citizens' Beliefs and Perceptions?" *Public Management* 87, no. 4 (2005): 20–23; quote at 20.

28. More information on the FBI's citizens academies can be found on the Community Outreach page of the Bureau's website at www.fbi.gov/about-us/partnerships_and_outreach/community_outreach/citizens_academies.

29. Joyce E. Bono, Winny Shen, and Mark Snyder, "Fostering Integrative Community Leadership." *Leadership Quarterly* 21, no. 2 (2010): 324–35; quote at 326.

30. Rex F. Galloway, "Community Leadership Programs: New Implications for Local Leadership Enhancement, Economic Development, and Benefits for Regional Industries." *Economic Development Review* 15, no. 2 (1997): 6–9.

knowledge, particularly in the form of increased awareness and understanding of local government. Perhaps the most important difference between CLPs and citizens academies is that citizens academies are almost always open to any resident (sometimes, though, requiring proof-of-residency or age), whereas CLPs are more selective and can even be by invitation only. Thus CLPs may rightfully be viewed as being more exclusive than citizens academies, which usually are much more inclusive.

What Citizens Academies Look Like

This section focuses on the common features of citizens academies and what they generally look like. Table 1.1 presents a snapshot of "typical" citizens academies in North Carolina[31] along with some features of outlier programs.

Purpose and Goals

Perhaps the most important question to ask is why local governments take the time and effort to establish and run citizens academies. What are the purposes and goals of such programs? What do local governments hope to accomplish through them? In examining program materials from dozens of programs and also by speaking with many program coordinators, we find that three broad themes stand out as the primary purposes and goals of citizens academies: (1) knowledge, (2) involvement, and (3) community relations (see Table 1.2). It is worth noting that these purposes and goals, broadly speaking, correspond with the historical purposes and goals of CPAs.[32] Again, the important difference here is the *enterprise-wide* versus *agency-specific* focus of citizens academies.

---

31. These general observations about citizens academies are based on North Carolina programs because, given our proximity and relationships with North Carolina local governments, we have more information on them. A national database of programs has been maintained by the UNC School of Government since 2011, and entries for programs in North Carolina far outnumber those of other states, again because of proximity and the ease of collecting information from municipalities and counties across this state. We have no reason to believe, however, that North Carolina programs are very different from others across the country and thus use our awareness of dozens of programs here to loosely generalize about programs nationwide.

32. Vic W. Bumphus, Larry K. Gaines, and Curt R. Blakely, "Citizen Police Academies: Observing Goals, Objectives, and Recent Trends." *American Journal of*

Table 1.1 Typical and Outlier Citizens Academies

Typical Citizens Academy Program	Exceptions to the Norm
Started recently (less than 10 years old).	Hickory's program launched in 1998.
Single local government, produced solely in-house.	The Durham Neighborhood College is a co-production of the City of Durham and Durham County.
Offered once annually, with an application process, a cohort group attending multiple sessions, and a graduation ceremony at the end.	Cabarrus County offers its County Government 101 as somewhat of an à la carte program, with one-day, hands-on sessions covering one topic and participants attending only those sessions they are interested in (i.e., no cohort, no series of sessions). Some cohort programs offer the program more than once a year.
Extensive curriculum covered over 8 to 10, 2- to 3-hour sessions.	Catawba County University is offered in two, longer (4-hour) sessions.
Numbers of applicants close enough to target enrollment such that usually everyone is accepted. Short waiting lists if necessary.	Some programs have much higher demand than available slots and have waiting lists each year.
Cohort of 20 to 25 participants.	Some (mostly smaller) communities report cohorts of 8 to 12 participants, with a few programs hosting cohorts of up to 50 participants.
Modest program budgets around $2,000 to cover food, materials, transportation, and "swag," such as T-shirts, mugs, etc.	Some budgets are larger, over $5,000, while others report budgets in the $200 to $400 range.

While each of these three themes is promoted to a considerable extent across all citizens academies, we find wide variation in terms of the extent to which a particular purpose and goal is advanced, from a very basic approach to more substantive or advanced efforts. Basic manifestations of these goals seem to correspond to programs that are more public relations oriented, whereas programs that promote more advanced or substantive versions of these goals seem more oriented toward *civic capacity building*. We believe this discussion is important, and instructive, as a simpler, more basic approach to citizens academies aligns more with traditional (more *transactional*, if you will) notions of citizen participation

Criminal Justice 24, no. 1 (1999): 67–79; Becton et al., "Can Citizen Police Academies Influence Citizens' Beliefs and Perceptions?"

Table 1.2   Purposes and Goals of Citizens Academies

Basic Goal	Advanced Manifestation—Emphasis on Capacity Building
Knowledge	
Equip citizens with basic information about their local government.	Help staff learn more about citizen perspectives on local government service.
Help citizens who participate in local government become better informed.	Citizens learn about key issues facing the community.
Involvement	
Encourage greater citizen involvement.	Explicitly prepare participants for service on boards and commissions.
Citizens learn how to get more involved in local government.	Cultivate community leadership within neighborhoods and the community at large.
Community Relations	
Participants get to know—and improve lines of communication with—public officials.	Participants engage in dialogue with other citizens and local government officials.
Participants become informal ambassadors for the local government out in the community.	Community building (social capital development) among participants as well as with staff.

while more advanced approaches correspond with an *engagement* orientation that is more *transformational*. Each theme is discussed below.

Knowledge

The first and most basic purpose of citizens academies is to improve participants' knowledge of local government. Local government officials recognize that the average citizen has a very limited understanding of what local governments do and how they do it. These officials see a need to educate the public generally about the public benefits produced by their county or municipality, and they view citizens academies as one way of offering that education.

There also is a perception among local government officials that citizens who become engaged in local decision-making processes are often too ill-informed about how things work to meaningfully participate.[33] In other words, while it may be admirable that citizens want to be involved, their involvement may be of little

---

33. Barnes and Mann, *Making Local Democracy Work*.

use if it is not informed involvement. Citizens academies are therefore seen, at the most basic level, as a means of cultivating better informed citizen participation. For example, one program description states: "The purpose of the Academy is to inform citizens about how their local government is organized and how services are funded and delivered through first-hand experience and exposure."

Some programs take this a step further and approach the knowledge dimension in more substantive ways. While acknowledging the importance of more citizens being better informed about what local government does and how it works, these citizens academies also seek to impart citizen input to staff members. An example of such a program is one which states that one of its purposes is to "obtain feedback from citizens regarding governmental programs and services."

Another more substantive manifestation of the knowledge-building goal involves programs that go beyond simply "familiarizing citizens with the structure, functions, and activities of local government" by including discussions of current issues the community is grappling with. Some programs specifically state that they inform citizens on "key issues" or that academy participants will better understand "what issues drive decisions." A few programs even specifically state that participants will engage in "dialogue," which suggests that mutual learning on issues is a goal in addition to more traditional one-way learning.

Involvement

The second stated purpose of citizens academies is to increase citizen involvement in local government. Program materials often mention that participants will "learn how citizens can be more involved with their government" or that participants will leave "better able to be involved." The most basic goal is to generate greater citizen involvement, with the implication that citizens who are involved in the program will be better equipped to be involved more broadly (thereby linking the first two goals).

Many programs take this goal a step further, however, and view citizens academies as a pipeline for substantial citizen involvement in the form of serving on boards, commissions, committees, and so forth. A typical program statement along these lines is that participants will have opportunities to "apply for openings on . . . boards and commissions." A Kissimmee, Florida, news release (September 4, 2013) noted that Kissimmee citizens academy "graduates have filled more than 90 positions on the City's advisory boards and volunteer committees."[34]

---

34. See www.kissimmee.org/index.aspx?recordid=870&page=31.

> *This experience was just wonderful. I really didn't know what to expect. As a new resident, I now feel that I know so much more about my "new home" than before. There was so much useful information presented. Thank you so much!*
>
> *Loved meeting the people! Now it no longer feels like "the City." Am very impressed with the sincerity and dedication of so many city leaders.*
>
> Comments from two 2011 graduates of Decatur (Georgia) 101

The pathway to involvement often does extend to elected positions. The Coconut Creek, Florida, Citizen's Academy notes on its program webpage that "ideally, some of these graduates will go on to run for elected office or sit on appointed boards."[35] We have heard (anecdotally) from several program contacts that some of their current elected board members are citizens academy graduates.

Related to this expanded or more advanced version of the involvement goal is the idea of leadership development. The sense here is that citizens are being prepared not only for community service but also, at least potentially, to take on broader leadership roles in their neighborhoods or communities. Thus you find some program materials including statements like "cultivating new community leaders" and providing participants with "the ability to be effective leaders in their neighborhoods."

While language about developing leaders is a common element of program materials, the curricula of citizens academies usually do not include content explicitly focusing on leadership development. Nonetheless, the stated goals of developing leadership point to the possibility of expanding curricula to go beyond the nuts and bolts of Local Government 101 to include some leadership development, perhaps in partnership with community or educational organizations equipped to conduct such training. Some of the programs engaged in partnerships to achieve this kind of programming are highlighted later in this handbook.

Community Relations

The third stated purpose of citizens academies is improving community relations. At its most basic level, this goal has to do with the value citizens place on getting to know local officials. Many programs cite "getting to know staff" and improving or promoting "open lines of communication" between citizens and staff as a primary goal. In addition, there is a very common notion that participants, as they get to

---

35. See www.coconutcreek.net/community-relations-folder/citizen's-academy.

know staff and see how the city is run, will become ambassadors of a sort for the local government out in the community. For example, a goal expressed by one program description is that participants "will bring their specialized knowledge of how city government works back to their respective neighborhoods." Another program description asserts that it has "turned adversaries into advocates."

The more advanced or substantive (that is, capacity building) manifestation of the community relations goal links back to the notion of engendering dialogue and the related idea of building community among participants and local government officials (appointed as well as elected). As noted above, some programs speak of creating opportunities for local officials and citizens to have dialogue on important issues, a process that builds common understanding and relationships. The Redwood City, California, Partnership Academy for Community Teamwork (PACT) program is exemplary in this respect, as it very deliberately avoids PowerPoint presentations and instead emphasizes community building among participants as well as among participants and city staff.[36] The PACT program is described as involving citizens "in helping to strengthen our community." The core idea is to break down an "us versus them" dynamic between citizens and city hall and transform it into a "we" characterized by a collaborative spirit through which everyone feels a part of the community-wide effort to improve the community.

As noted above, there is a remarkable consistency across all programs we have examined in terms of these three purposes being expressed in some way. The variation lies in the extent to which each goal is expressed or, rather, how *advanced* or *substantive* they are in terms of building capacity for civic engagement. All programs speak in terms of knowledge development—that participants will learn about how local government works. Some go a step further, however, and emphasize knowledge sharing in both directions. Most programs include some amount of information regarding opportunities for citizens to get involved in their community, while others seek more substantive involvement, actively encouraging "alumni" to apply for positions on boards or to become neighborhood leaders. Finally, all programs have a community relations element, in the hope that participants will become ambassadors for the organization within the community. A few take this idea a step further and see the program as an opportunity to *build community* among participants as well as with staff.

---

36. Ed Everett, "Community Building: How to Do It, Why It Matters," *ICMA IQ Report* 41, no. 4 (2009): 1–14.

Participants in the Cary (N.C.) School of Government learning about public works and building relationships with public works employees (Photo by Bruce Rosar)

Based on our examination of dozens of programs, we offer the following propositions about citizens academies and building capacity for civic engagement:

1. Citizens academies can improve the skills and knowledge of citizens with respect to engaging in community affairs.
2. The more citizens academies emphasize avenues and opportunities for participation, the greater impact they will have on developing leadership and active participation among citizens.
3. The more citizens academies facilitate community building and dialogue, the more impact they will have on developing the social capital and "spaces for dialogue and collective action" dimensions of civic capacity.

It is also important to note that there may be second- and third-order benefits in terms of civic capacity building that, while difficult to measure, are nevertheless vitally important. For example, dialogue and community building activities might lay the groundwork for partnerships outside of those between citizens and

Table 1.3   Common Problems in Community Engagement and How Citizens Academies Address Them

Problem	How Citizens Academies Help
Uninformed citizenry.	Equip citizens with basic knowledge about how local government works, what services are delivered, how they're delivered, etc.
Low levels of involvement (participants tend to be the "usual suspects").	Cultivate more interest in being involved and broaden the pool of "active" citizens.
Negative attitudes about government and poor relationships between local government and citizens generally speaking.	Community building and relationship development among public officials and citizens.

local government officials that are nevertheless beneficial to the civic health of the community. Learning about local government and building relationships with staff may create better informed and more involved citizens in the near term while also contributing to generalized public trust in the long term.

Citizens academies are becoming more and more common throughout the United States. These programs hold significant promise in terms of developing local community civic infrastructure, that is, the capacity for more meaningful civic engagement. Linda Harris, coordinator of Decatur 101, the Atlanta suburb's very popular citizens academy, estimated that 70 percent of those attending the kick-off session of the community's strategic planning process were graduates of the program. She also noted that the program helps to generate hundreds of enthusiastic volunteers for a variety of community events, some sponsored by government and others by non-profits. The impact of citizens academies can be significant (see Table 1.3).

It is worth noting, though, that not all citizens academies are as successful as Decatur 101, the Cary School of Government, or Clearwater 101. Some programs have shut down after a few years due to limited demand or lack of support. We believe, however, that the potential exists within virtually any local government to establish a successful program. There must be a champion within the organization and support from upper management and elected officials. There must also be genuine, organization-wide commitment to civic engagement and citizen empowerment. No one wants to waste their time on a public relations showcase; indeed, a program that is just for show is likely to do more harm than good. Our recommendation for organizations that offer a citizens academy or are considering offering one is that *every effort be made to maximize its potential for civic capacity building.* We hope that the tips and tools provided by this handbook will help local governments reach that goal.

Questions to Consider

What is your organization's commitment to civic engagement, in terms of both staff and the elected board?

_____

_____

What is your organization's commitment to building capacity for civic engagement? What efforts are currently being made to develop the capacity of local citizens to engage in community efforts more broadly and with their local government specifically? How might a citizens academy align with organizational goals around building civic capacity?

_____

_____

_____

_____

Does your organization have the available resources to start a program?

_____

_____

For organizations that are considering offering a citizens academy, how would its purposes and goals be articulated?

_____

_____

For organizations that are already operating a citizens academy, what are its goals and objectives? To what extent do its goals point toward civic capacity building?

_____

_____

2. Getting Started: Objectives, Curriculum, and Logistical Considerations

> *I was amazed at what it takes to run the city, and I was very impressed with the leaders of our city. I tell folks in the community that you have no idea just how well this city runs and how dedicated the folks in charge are.*
>
> 2010 Graduate of the Greensboro (North Carolina) City Academy

After determining clear purposes and goals for the program, the team (or point person) must next determine how to design the citizens academy so that it will fit the community's particular situation. The *what* (as in, what should the program include) will determine the *who* (as in, who needs to be involved in program design). Locking down these essential elements of the overall plan will determine other key logistics, such as where and when the sessions will take place as well as how much time participants (and staff) will be expected to dedicate to the program.

Creating Clear Learning Objectives and Outcomes

As noted in Chapter 1, it is important that a citizens academy be based on a clear set of goals. We noted that the three meta-goals of knowledge, involvement, and community relations are common across virtually all programs. We also emphasized the importance of realizing the civic capacity building potential within each of these themes. Programs that fail to generate positive word of mouth will likely not get beyond transmitting information. Successful programs create opportunities for mutual learning, inspire citizens to serve their community, and build social capital along the way.

For organizations with a clear set of system-wide strategic goals and objectives, it is important to link the effort involved in conducting a citizens academy with those larger organizational goals. This is not only good management practice (to align activity with strategic goals), but it also can help ensure long-term commitment from "the top." Many, if not most, local governments in the United States have established some strategic goals around citizen engagement, so it should not be hard to link program objectives with larger organizational goals and objectives.

Creating learning objectives is another important component of any kind of educational program. In formal educational settings, learning objectives usually refer to what topics will be covered. For a citizens academy, the notion of developing learning outcomes goes a step further to refer to the knowledge, skills, and abilities (KSAs) that participants should have upon completion of the course or program. In other words, what will participants know and be able to do after the program is over?

Program purposes, goals, and outcomes can and should shape more specific objectives in terms of thinking about what topics should be covered. They can also provide guidance for programmatic questions, such as whether it is important that participants attend all sessions, or most of them, or whether it is okay for people to simply attend sessions as they please. While some programs allow participants to miss one or two sessions, many will not allow participants to graduate unless they have attended all sessions, with perhaps some allowance given for extraordinary circumstances or for providing opportunities for makeup sessions. Attendance requirements can serve specific learning outcomes in terms of what academy graduates should know as well as be a factor in reaching the goal of building social capital within a cohort.

Determining the Scope of a Program's Curriculum

In order to determine the scope and structure of a program, coordinators and/or planning committees must consider the key government functions, community partners, and particulars of the community that might be of particular interest to participants. A citizens academy is an opportunity to highlight local government

Developing Clear Program Goals/Objectives

The example of Hillsborough, North Carolina, is instructive. In alignment with the town-wide balanced scorecard, the Hillsborough Citizens Academy was created to "support development of citizen volunteers." Together with input from the town board and staff, Town Manager Eric Peterson developed the following four objectives for the program:

1. increase citizen knowledge, interest, and ability to influence as well as participate in town government;

2. reduce barriers to participating in and influencing town government decisions through increased understanding of key processes and operations;

3. assist in building a pipeline of citizens interested in serving the community in the future (e.g., sharing of perspectives during public hearings, participating in neighborhood watch associations, advocating for key issues, serving on advisory committees, volunteer town boards, and the Hillsborough Board of Commissioners);

4. learning from the citizens attending the academy.

Note how these program objectives constitute both a concise description of the overall purposes and goals for the program as well as desired outcomes (increase knowledge, interest, and ability as they relate to participating with the town government).

successes and to show citizens what happens behind the scenes. The following are several questions to consider:

- What are you most proud of? What part of your work do you want to feature?
- What programs and facilities do you have to offer that are unique?
- What hidden gems (facilities, programs) are there that you would like to get more exposure for?
- What issues are hot topics within the community?
- What aspects of local government do citizens need to know but are often misunderstood?

While coordinators and those on planning committees might have a compre-hensive understanding of an organization, most citizens know very little about local government. Thus, it could be helpful to seek input from external and internal stakeholders in order to gain clarity on what aspects of the organization are essential to feature when developing a well-rounded, comprehensive curriculum. Such input can be gathered in various ways, including the following:

- Discuss goals and learning outcomes for the program with the governing board.
- Put together a focus group of key staff within the organization and hold a brainstorming session.
- Solicit one-on-one input from department heads whose departments are being considered for inclusion in programming.
- Conduct a focus group or have informal conversations with citizens.
- Send out a quick email survey to make providing feedback easy.

Some programs even create advisory boards/committees for the program made up of alumni. (This will be discussed in more detail in Chapter 5.) Such arrangements certainly represent a method of gaining insight into learning objectives and outcomes that takes citizen engagement seriously.

Reviewing Common Session Topics

Agendas for citizens academies are remarkably similar across the country. Some, though, are more extensive than others. Concord (North Carolina) 101, for example, has added several new sessions over the years due to participant demand. Some programs even build flexibility into the curriculum so that participants can identify topics they want to cover in future sessions. Other programs stick to essentially the exact same agenda for each program but mix up the content within each session according to the feedback they receive. The key of course is to ensure that timely and relevant issues are covered, which means that at least minor adjustments will need to be made to the agenda from year to year.

Most session topics correspond to city or county functional units and departments. As such, coordinators (usually in the public information or manager's office) organize the sessions and shepherd participants through the program but usually do very little teaching. Most sessions are taught by individual department or division heads and usually cover topics in a manner similar to examples given in this chapter and in the exhibit items presented in Appendix 2.

The initial session for most programs provides a summary of government organization and structure, and community history as well as introductions by key public officials and administrators. Providing a basic overview is important because, as has been noted, most citizens know very little about local government. Helpful

---

Sample Municipal Agenda: Alexandria (Virginia) Fall 2014 City Academy

- *Session No. 1*—Welcome, introductions, history of Alexandria, organizational chart, communications and public information, human rights, Alexandria City Public Schools System
- *Session No. 2*—Economic development, city offices of housing, planning and zoning
- *Session No. 3*—Fire and emergency management services
- *Session No. 4*—Community and human services
- *Session No. 5*—City financial management
- *Session No. 6*—Code administration, transportation, and environmental services
- *Session No. 7*—Office of human resources, city judicial system, general services, information technology services
- *Session No. 8*—Leisure and cultural activities
- *Session No. 9*—Public safety (police and sheriff)

---

overviews are available through the National League of Cities (see www.nlc.org/ build-skills-and-networks/resources/cities-101) and the National Association of Counties (see www.naco.org/counties-matter). The International City/County Management Association's Life Well Run initiative (see www.lifewellrun.org) has developed many helpful resources, such as videos and even a Prezi presentation titled Local Government 101, that could be used in an introductory session or even as homework for a citizens academy.

Other programs, such as the Fort Smith (Arkansas) Citizens Academy, open with a more interactive exercise—in this case, a tour of the downtown area. Beginning with an interactive and relationship building session may be more in line with community building goals, but at some point early on, an overview of the community and local government, including introductions to key people, should be included in the agenda, as this will help set the stage for the rest of the program.

For the final session, some programs choose to focus on a predetermined topic followed by a graduation event of some kind. Others, as mentioned above, allow participants to determine the subject based on collective feedback (done in Catawba County, North Carolina, for example). Some final sessions are held during board meetings during which graduates are publicly recognized. (A fuller discussion of graduation events is provided in Chapter 5.)

Helpful Resources for Introducing Local Government to Participants

National League of Cities (NLC), www.nlc.org/build-skills-and-networks/resources/cities-101

National Association of Counties (NACo), www.naco.org/counties-matter

Life, Well Run (initiative of the International City/County Management Association (ICMA)), www.lifewellrun.org

ICMA Council–Manager Form Resource Page, www.icma.org/en/Page/100086/ CouncilManager_Form_Resource_Package

Resources available through state Leagues of Municipalities or Associations of Counties

Sample County Agenda: Rockingham County (North Carolina) Fall 2012 Citizens Academy

- *Session No. 1*—Welcome, introduction, and county government organizational chart
- *Session No. 2*—County history, geography, population, culture, and SWOT analysis (strength, weaknesses, opportunities, and threats)
- *Session No. 3*—Human resources, safety/risk, legal, information technology, public information
- *Session No. 4*—Public health, engineering and public utilities, soil and water conservation, code enforcement, animal shelter
- *Session No. 5*—Social services, veterans services, youth services, Head Start
- *Session No. 6*—Cooperative extension, business and technology, economic and tourism development
- *Session No. 7*—Board of elections and library
- *Session No. 8*—Law enforcement, fire, emergency management, 9-1-1 communications, emergency medical services, pre-trial services
- *Session No. 9*—Register of deeds, planning/inspections, geographic information systems, tax administration
- *Session No. 10*—Budget, finance, purchasing, lean management

What Logistical Aspects Should Be Considered in Planning the Program?

Once a municipality or county decides to conduct a citizens academy and articulates the goals and desired outcomes of that program, the logistics necessary for accomplishing these goals becomes the next consideration. Staff coordinators, as well as any program partners, must agree on a time of year, set a regular schedule, reserve a meeting space, and ensure that there are ample resources to cover program needs. The various determinations made over the course of the implementation phase will differ from program to program according to how coordinators go about linking the program to organizational and communitywide goals.

As the following sections demonstrate, successful programs focus on what works best for their individual communities. For instance, program intervals will affect the ability of some citizens to attend. This section offers examples and suggestions for both common scheduling and flexible or alternative scheduling used by the programs we have reviewed.

Meeting days and times constitute another logistical consideration that should be decided carefully so as to maximize the number of participants. The same goes for the location of each session. Coordinators need to consider the benefits and drawbacks of holding citizen academy sessions at specific locations around town, which could necessitate exploring locales other than city hall. Finally, budgets should be finalized as soon as possible so as to set expectations throughout the program planning and implementation phases.

Deciding the Session Intervals
Common Scheduling

Most programs are conducted at least once (sometimes twice) per year. Fall sessions, from September to November, or spring terms, spanning February to April, are most common. Offering programs during these months often prevents major conflicts with holidays, severe weather, and late-spring budget processes.

Program coordinators should consider using departmental activities held throughout the year as teachable moments for academy participants. For instance, an election year provides a great opportunity for participants to become informed about the local electoral process and how it shapes the leadership of their community. If a program aligns with the end of a fiscal year, participants can learn about local budgetary responsibilities and experience the end-of-year budgeting process from a legislative and administrative perspective.

Some communities time their programs to help achieve the goal of increased citizen engagement. The Cary (North Carolina) School of Government, for example, schedules sessions in either the fall or spring, whichever season immediately precedes the application period for serving on town boards and commissions, so that recent alumni can apply for some of these positions. Discussed more in Chapter 5, Cary's deliberate timing provides an excellent example of linking scheduling decisions with program goals.

Flexible Scheduling

Some programs advertise themselves as being offered on an "as-needed" basis. In some cases, this means that a citizens academy is held when local government leaders feel it is needed, which does not mean at regular intervals. In other cases, "as-needed" means that a city or county will accommodate a citizens group or church or other community organization that would like to host an academy by essentially putting on a customized program for them (Bend, Oregon, for example, advertises it's Bend 101 citizens academy this way).

Flexible scheduling certainly has its advantages. There is the chance, however, that citizens will view it as government trying to avoid or curb opposition to, or to build support for, a particular issue, such as an upcoming vote on a bond referendum. Some program coordinators have reported success with conducting their programs irregularly, as needed—due to insufficient citizen interest in an annual program, for example—but there are other ways to address this challenge. The Addison (Texas) Citizens Academy, for instance, provides a good example of a condensed program that is suited to being offered at various times (see the sidebar spotlighting the Addison program).

Accommodating Citizens' Schedules

While most communities offer programs once a year at a set time, some adjust their offerings to meet the realities of their community and the needs of their residents. Communities such as Martin County, Florida, cater to a robust population of older adults who enjoy spending their winters in a warmer climate. The county's Citizens Academy & Resource Education Series (Martin CARES) holds multiple programs each year during the fall and winter months, typically for six weeks at a time with half- to full-day sessions occurring once weekly on a weekday. The number of program sessions held throughout the year is determined by available resources and citizen interest. Martin County is unique in that it has the budget for and enough citizen interest in offering the program to up to 50 participants each session.

Spotlight on the Addison (Texas) Citizens Academy

Addison, Texas, a town with a population of around 13,000 located on the outskirts of Dallas, created a citizens academy in 2000 "to provide a curriculum for the purpose of fostering a greater sense of understanding of the Town of Addison and all its municipal functions in a fun and interactive forum."

The town offers its program as three day-long sessions in order to ensure ample participation at each session. About 30 to 35 people making up a cross section of Addison residents learn about government structure, public works, and public safety functions, among other topics, over three consecutive Saturdays. The instruction is comprehensive but incorporates elements of hands-on learning

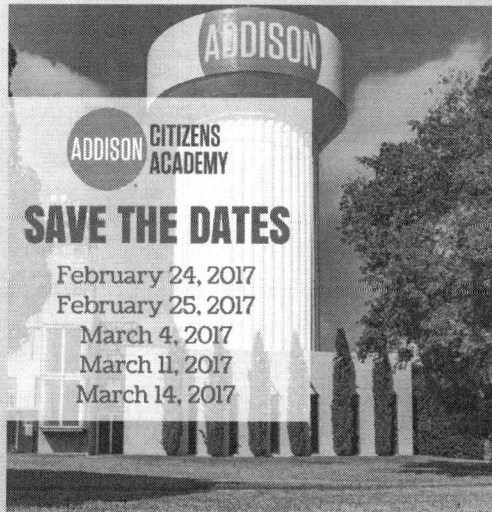

through special project assignments associated with certain topics. In addition to the day-long sessions, participants have opportunities outside of these meetings to get to know their peers, the support staff, and elected officials. The sessions are flanked by two dinner events (one opening the program, the other closing it) and attendance at a reception held at an Addison City Council meeting is required.

After six sessions of the program, 11 graduates had put their learning into practice by serving on town council or running for mayor. Many other program alumni have gone on to serve on appointed boards or commissions.

> *What I took away from this Academy experience was an increased respect and appreciation for the open and close inter-working of all those involved with Town and County Government positions that share in services, ideas, facilities, equipment and manpower for the benefit of the public. I now have a better understanding of just how much planning, work and dedication actually go into trying to make everything "just right," safe and enjoyable for everyone in the community.*
>
> Montgomery County–Christiansburg Citizens Academy participant

Deciding the Number of Sessions

A typical citizens academy consists of around 8 sessions. The number of sessions ranges from as few as 3 to 5 to as many as 12 or even 16 (Raleigh and Concord, North Carolina, respectively). But 8 to 10 is the norm. Sessions are usually held weekly over the course of two to three months. However, a few programs hold monthly sessions—from October through May in the case of the Southern Pines (North Carolina) Citizens Academy, for example. Ultimately, the number of sessions should depend on participant interest, local government objectives, and resources available to it.

Deciding the Time of Sessions

Time of day also is an important consideration. The norm is to hold sessions on a set evening and, depending on the length of the session, provide a light meal or at least snacks. For instance, sessions of the Clearwater, Florida, citizens academy are held weekly on weekday nights from 6:00 to 8:30 p.m. As demonstrated by the robust interest shown by residents from year to year, this format works well for participants who cannot attend weekday sessions due to work or other obligations. The two-and-a-half hour meeting is held every Tuesday for 10 weeks and includes time for a light supper.

However, many programs, after considering feedback from citizens and academy alumni on how to bolster interest and attendance, have begun to offer sessions at different times. Some programs meet fewer times for longer periods while others limit sessions to a single weekend, a format that reduces program costs by covering every topic in a short, but intensive, time frame.

Some programs have been successful holding classes during business hours, with the obvious tradeoff being that it severely limits the number of participants who can attend. Evening programs also can limit accessibility, though, especially in communities where many residents work the second or third shift. Evenings can be difficult also for single parents. Some programs are large enough to be able to offer multiple options. Decatur, Georgia, for example, has enough

Spotlight on Davidson (North Carolina) Civics 101

Civics 101 is offered every spring for nine weeks. In essence, the town offers two simultaneous programs. The nine sessions of each program are held on consecutive Thursdays—one from 9:30–11:30 a.m. and one from 6:30–8:00 p.m.—not including a Saturday field trip and the graduation ceremony at a regular meeting of the Davidson County Board of Commissioners. Participants can elect to attend either the morning or the evening session, depending on their schedules. Due to consistently high citizen interest (there usually is a short waiting list) and a capped enrollment of 25 for each program, town staff determined that this schedule structure is the least taxing on presenters' time and serves twice as many participants at once.

Town staff generate much of the interest in this program by recruiting via word of mouth, social media, the town website, outreach to individual residents, and solicitations from the town board. Participants are selected on a first-come, first-served basis.

The program is free for all, and light snacks and coffee are provided. Program materials note that "participants should not expect nine weeks of lectures," as classes "require participation in discussion and activities, and sessions often rotate among town facilities." In addition to the graduation certificate, participants receive a commemorative mug. Such minimal expenses enable the town to spend about $500 or less each year on running the academy. Even without spending thousands on the program, the town achieves its citizen participation goals: graduates have served as elected commissioners, and many alumni have served in appointed capacities.

participants each year to have both daytime and evening tracks. Davidson, North Carolina, is similar; it conducts one program per year (January–March) but with two session options, 9:30–11:30 a.m. and 6–9 p.m., for seven consecutive Thursdays.

Martin CARES (mentioned above) is another program that sets its schedule according to the availability of county residents. In order to accommodate the snowbirds who reside in the area during the winter months, CARES hosts a program characterized by much longer sessions, running for six consecutive Thursdays from 7:45 a.m.–3:00 p.m.

The day itself also requires careful consideration. It is also important to consider nights with many official government meetings (i.e., boards, councils, etc.). Some dates also present scheduling conflicts with religious obligations for some community members. Tuesdays and Thursdays are the most common days selected. Saturday mornings are frequently reserved for community or facility tours.

The à la carte Approach to Programming

Not all citizens academies bring in cohorts that are committed to attend all (or most) sessions, offered in sequential format, with a graduation at the end. Some programs offer what are called citizens academies, but more in what might be considered an à la carte format. Take, for example, Cabarrus County, North Carolina. Its "County Government 101" used to follow the norm, being a 10-week course touching all aspects of county government. Participants applied and were admitted as a cohort, as the vast majority of programs do. The program transformed to a new format that offers one-day sessions that delve deep into one area of focus. The sessions are hands-on and experiential. Class sizes are limited to 20 participants, and registration is required. But there is no commitment to take a certain number of classes, and classes are not offered in any particular sequence or regular interval.

Of course, local governments should weigh the flexibility benefit of this à la carte option against potential drawbacks to not requiring that citizens commit themselves to a longer program. One concern is participants may not have the opportunity to bond with their cohort or government staff if they are only spending time with each other at these one-day sessions. As discussed in Chapter 1, community relations and even network-building is one of the main purposes of having a citizens academy and getting to learn and grow with one another over the course of multiple weeks is one of the ways to ensure people (and local government practitioners) get to participate in this important goal.

Another drawback hits on the goal of providing an opportunity for citizens to acquire knowledge about local government issues, as discussed in Chapter 1. A single day session may not be enough time to go in-depth into some of the more intricate issues that are critical for understanding the community they live and work in. Ultimately, in considering an à la carte approach to citizens academies, program staff should discuss among themselves whether the program's purpose is to give citizens a quick taste of local government, or if they are looking to provide an opportunity for citizens to bond with one another and staff, as well as gain more in-depth knowledge about their communities. The former would warrant a single-day format like Cabarrus County's, but the latter might want to consider sticking with the longer format.

The City of Charlotte, North Carolina, has had a more-or-less à la carte program for many years. Its "Community University" is described this way on the charmeck.org website:

> Community University is a neighborhood capacity building program dedicated to providing high quality training to Charlotte residents to improve the strength and vitality of neighborhood organizations and businesses to enhance the overall quality of community life.
>
> The courses are intended to engage, inform, and equip participants with the training and assistance needed to help them improve and maintain Charlotte's communities and business corridors.

The courses are free and open to any interested resident. Typically there is one topic per month with four sessions/workshops that form a series around that topic. There is an application for individual classes and for month-long series, but no graduation or expectation that participants attend all the classes in a series or all the series offered during the course of year.

Another variation on the à la carte approach can be found in the Garland (Texas) Neighborhood Management Academy (GNMA). According to its website at garlandtx.gov, the GNMA "offers educational classes on a variety of topics important to neighborhood vitality. Categories include citizen engagement, leadership development, and neighborhood management." The classes offered go well beyond "local government 101" topics, surveying different departments and whatnot. There is a course called "City Government 101" that is a three-hour overview of city government operations. Most of the other courses, however, are more explicitly about capacity building, with leadership development offerings such as communication, conflict resolution, and volunteer recruitment.

The GNMA has a much more neighborhood-leadership focus than most programs. The important distinction here though is that the different classes, offered regularly on Thursday evenings and Saturday mornings, can be taken as stand-alone courses, with no commitment to take others. Registration is required to help plan for class size.

GNMA adds one interesting wrinkle to the à la carte approach though. They offer a certification program, where people can get certifications in one of three areas of concentration: citizen engagement, leadership development, and neighborhood management. In order to get certified, one must first take the City Government 101 (introductory) class, then complete five more courses within a track. This appears to be a promising middle-ground between the pure à la carte approach and the more rigid, traditional approach which usually requires a commitment to attend a lot of classes over a short period of time.

Setting Aside a Budget

Program Fees?

While most programs are provided at no cost for residents, some communities charge a nominal fee to each participant. For those that chose to assess fees, they are usually around $25 and usually do not cover the full program costs. It is likewise common to provide scholarships for participants who need assistance (the Durham Neighborhood College and the Chatham County Citizens' College—both in North Carolina—are examples of this, charging nominal fees but providing scholarships essentially to anyone who asks).

The rationale behind charging fees is that if participants are required to invest their own money, consistent participation across the entire program will be more likely (i.e., "having skin in the game"). Of course the reason most do not charge a fee is so that cost is not a barrier and that it is seen as a service provided by the city rather than a fee-based program like one would find in the recreation department. There are good arguments for either approach, and again, program purposes and goals should inform the decision.

Deciding on a Program Budget

Like any program, large or small, it is important to work with a budget (usually within a departmental budget). Most programs do not have their own line-item in the organization's budget. Typically, the costs are low enough that a portion of the public information or city/county manager's budget can be set aside for this purpose. Not counting staff time (which most, if not all programs, do not try and

DIY table arrangements for Concord (N.C.) 101
(Photo by Cherie Jzar)

Touring a facility as part of Concord (N.C.) 101.
A hallmark of this long-running very well attended
program is that sessions are held at multiple
locations within the community.

quantify), programs typically spend between $1,000 and $2,000. The higher end of budgets we surveyed were between $5,000 and $6,000 and typically were in larger jurisdictions. On the lower end, we have seen many reported budgets of $400 or less.

Most of the money budgeted for citizens' academies is spent on the following:

- course materials (binders, documents, maps, etc.),
- food (catered dinners, snacks, refreshments, and graduation receptions),
- transportation (chartered buses or vans for facility tours), and
- participant gifts (paperweights, polo shirts, class photos, etc.).

In addition, nearly all programs provide participants with a binder of assembled information, including agendas, contact sheets, department information, and so on, often printed in-house at little cost. Providing electronic copies of the course packet is another option, as is done by the citizens academy in Hillsborough, North Carolina. Some organizers instruct presenting departments to prepare their own meals (such as the ever-popular firehouse chili) if the program does not provide a regular lunch or dinner. Finally, snacks and refreshments are sometimes provided at sessions, and most graduation events feature catered dinners or heavy hors d'oeuvres.

Population (community size) influences how much money is spent on the academy. Examining a sample of programs revealed that communities with a large population tend to spend more than those with fewer residents. Naturally, there is also a relationship between the amount of money spent on a program and the number of sessions included in it.

Choosing the Right Locations

Many communities hold sessions in facilities that are unique to them, such as community colleges, libraries, and recreation centers. However, while some communities hold their sessions in city hall or the county board meeting room, many others seek to vary the session location as much as possible. For instance, a session on public works might be hosted at the public works garage or operations center. A community recreation–focused session might include a visit to the parks and recreation department as well as presentations by relevant citizen advisory boards and community non-profits.

Locating sessions at various locations seems to refresh participant interest as it offers a more hands-on or experiential approach to learning about community and local government. At the most basic level, changing locations can help residents get to know different facilities within their community and feel more comfortable there. The idea of experiential learning, as discussed further in Chapter 4,

Spotlight on Gainesville (Florida) 101

Gainesville 101 runs for six weeks, beginning in March and October of each year, from 8:30 a.m. to noon on Wednesdays. Sessions cover such topics as the police department, the fire/rescue department, area utilities, and the structure and function of local government. (The program's website is at http://academy.cityofgainesville.org.)

Classes are limited to 40 people, and citizens are enrolled on a first-come, first-served basis. The program leads its peers in terms of its use of online resources. Applications and a list of board/commission openings are posted

2016 participants of Gainesville 101

on the city website. Also provided online is a comprehensive schedule that identifies the subject for a given week's session, the meeting time, and a Google map to the location.

In 2007, session participants created a blog about attending the program. Students write about their experiences, post pictures from the sessions, and access information regarding each session as well as relevant links provided in each presentation.

The Gainesville 101 graduation, held at a meeting of the city commission, features an address by a class-elected speaker.

stands in stark contrast to programs that rely primarily on lectures and PowerPoint presentations.

Like many programs, Winston-Salem, North Carolina, holds classes at multiple locations in addition to city hall: the public safety training center, an employee training center, a water treatment plant, and a recreation center. Concord (North Carolina) 101 takes this aspect a step further by providing a detailed map to guide participants to the various sites where classes will be held throughout the 15-week program (see Exhibit 2.4 in Appendix 2). While the first two sessions of Concord 101 take place at city hall, the rest are spread out across many municipal landmarks in all corners of the town, including the Concord Regional Airport, the Neighborhood Network Technology Center, and police headquarters. Although holding sessions at more than one location requires more planning, it is worth considering, as most participants would otherwise not have the opportunity to explore these facilities.

Garner (North Carolina) 101 is a good example of a program that recognizes the importance of incorporating a multitude of diverse experiences into the curriculum. As a way of complementing the curriculum it offers on the town and its services, program coordinators invite departments such as the Parks, Recreation and Cultural Resources Department, the Garner Police Department, Raleigh Public Utilities, and Garner Volunteer Fire-Rescue, Inc., to present at various sessions. Classes also include on-site facility tours and displays. As part of the attendance requirement, participants must be present for seven out of the nine scheduled sessions and attend a town council meeting prior to graduation. In addition, the program strongly encourages "homework" for participants in the form of taking the initiative to explore the town on their own time. These out-of-class activities could include going on a police ride-along, attending a parks, recreation, and cultural resources event, or downloading the free Garner Info mobile app.

Obviously transportation costs and logistics must be considered when deciding to vary session locations around the community. The program must be able to transport participants to the various locations, or the community must have adequate public transportation, or participants must have their own means of getting to the facilities.

Avoiding "Invisible Walls"

Whatever locations are chosen, programs should strive to ensure that they are accessible to all. The reality, though, is that oftentimes "invisible walls" present barriers to minorities or disabled persons. In her 1996 book *Bridging the Class Divide and Other Lessons for Grassroots Organizing*, Linda Stout explains that many well-intentioned people want to be inclusive and break down existing social barriers but often are unaware of how they themselves erect what amount to "invisible walls." And sometimes organizers are aware of the invisible walls but do not understand how to overcome them.

Program staff should be especially careful to avoid erecting invisible walls when working out the details of offering their program content to the community. Meetings need to be held in locations where all citizens feel comfortable, especially those attendees who traditionally have been excluded or marginalized by the larger society. For example, some participants might view the local police station as a threatening environment. Holding meetings at a local church or other facility owned by a faith-based organization could deter those of other faiths or who hold no religious belief from attending the sessions. The objective for staff throughout the program should be to nudge citizens to feel more comfortable inside public spaces while realizing that some locations or situations could present unintended barriers.

Another thing to keep in mind is that some attendees may need the locale to be wheelchair accessible, so staff will want to ensure that buildings where sessions are held have an ADA-accessible ramp and other accommodations if needed. Finally, working out the logistics of providing transportation to and from the meeting location is just as critical as deciding on the location itself. If some people do not have a vehicle and cannot conceivably reach the destination via public transportation, organizers could unintentionally keep out people who otherwise could have been important contributors to the academy experience. The same might be true for those who need childcare. These and other logistical factors that can either build or tear down invisible walls need to be considered in setting the scene for a citizens academy. Some early, heads-up planning can help minimize the building of invisible walls that may keep some citizens from even considering participating.

Running a citizens academy that will be accessible and worthwhile for members of the community requires open-mindedness, creativity, and dedication. Although it might be tempting to jump right into the more active stages of recruitment and implementation, a multitude of logistical factors, including the curriculum and logistics behind conducting the program, should be worked out beforehand if the program is to be successful down the road.

As discussed earlier in this chapter, one tip for getting started is to envision how the larger mission of the local government and community can be reflected in how the program operates. Taking a moment to reflect on overall organizational values and goals will serve as a guide once it is time to begin outlining program topics, the number and timing of sessions, a budget, and meeting locations. The next chapter focuses on the importance of recruiting diverse groups of people to sign up for citizens academies and presents some approaches to navigating the application and selection processes.

Questions to Consider

What are the established missions, goals, objectives and/or values by which your organization measures its overall performance?

_____

_____

How could these missions, goals, objectives and/or values be directly linked to what is offered in a citizens academy?

_____

_____

Who else should be consulted when making logistical decisions, either from within your organization or among community partners or community members?

_____

_____

What about your local government are you most proud of and think would be of interest to feature in the program?

_____

_____

What current events or issues are hot topics within the community that the program should either address or avoid?

_____

_____

What key concepts of local governance and management should citizens know about but could find difficult to understand?

_____

_____

What program format will best meet overall program goals and learning outcomes as well as the needs of the organization and the staff who will need to dedicate time and energy to the citizens academy?

_____

_____

2. Getting Started: Objectives, Curriculum, and Logistical Considerations

What meeting times will be most accommodating to the majority of citizens so as to increase the likelihood that community members from all backgrounds have the ability to participate?

_____

_____

What is the budget for the citizens academy? Where might you get the most "bang for your buck" in terms of program dollars?

_____

_____

What programs and facilities does your town or county have to offer that are unique and amenable to all participants?

_____

_____

What invisible walls to access might you inadvertently be putting up through the planning process (time, location, format, etc.)? How might you remove or at least lessen the impact of such walls so that the program can be as inclusive as possible?

_____

_____

Appendix 2   Exhibit Items

Exhibit 2.1   Alexandria (Virginia) City Academy Schedule

CURRICULUM FOR ALEXANDRIA CITY ACADEMY
(For Residents and Businesses)

The Alexandria City Academy is a nine (9) week program designed to offer our residents (over the age of 18) and business owners (located within the city limits) the opportunity to learn how their local government works and how they can become involved in the City.

Participants will learn about the many responsibilities and functions of the City Government, the relationships between the City Departments and the community and how services are provided. The Academy's goal is to educate the public and to increase awareness about what their local government does for them, provide an inside look into government operations, and to develop a better understanding of their role in city government.

The Graduation Ceremony will be held during a November City Council Legislative Meeting.

Session 1: Getting to Know Your City Government
September 10   City Hall - Council Workroom – 301 King Street
- Welcome
- Meet the Mayor and the City Manager
  - Overview of the Government Organization
- Council-Appointed Boards & Commissions
- Brief History of Alexandria
- Office of Communications & Public Information
- City Employment
- Voter Registration

Session 2: Community Development
September 17   City Hall - Council Workroom
- Promoting the City's Economic Development
  - Visiting Alexandria
  - Alexandria Economic Development Partnership (AEDP)
- Housing and Housing Related Programs
- Planning & Zoning – Process and Principles

Session 3: Public Safety - Fire
September 24   Fire Administration - Station 204 - 900 Second Street
- Emergency Preparedness
- Fire and EMS Services

Exhibit 2.1   Alexandria (Virginia) City Academy Schedule (*continued*)

Session 4:   General Services
October 1   Finance and Support Services
                  Office of Management and Budget (OMB)
                      City Hall - Council Workroom
- General Services
- Finance Department
  - o Overview
  - o Overview 2015 Real Estate Assessments
- Overview of the City's Operating and Capital Improvement Program (CIP) Budgets
- Overview of Budget Process – FY '17

Session 5   Community and Human Services
October 8   Alexandria Department of Health - 4480 King Street
- Public Health
- Department of Community and Human Services

Session 6:   Leisure and Cultural Activities
October 15   Charles Houston Center – 901 Wythe Street
- Parks & Recreation
- Alexandria City Library
- Historic Sites and Museums

Session 7:   Code Administration
October 22   Transportation and Environmental Services
                      City Hall - Council Workroom
- Department of Code Administration
  - o Building Controls/Code Enforcement
- Transportation and Environmental Services
  - o Transportation Policy
  - o Traffic Management System
  - o Transit Services
  - o DASH
  - o Street Maintenance
  - o Garbage Collection and Recycling
  - o Environmental Quality Controls

Session 8:   Office of Human Rights
October 29   The City's Judicial System
                  Information Technology (ITS)
                      City Hall - Council Workroom
- Human Rights
- Panel discussion with members of the City's Judicial System
- Information and Technology Services

Session 9:   Public Safety - Police and Sheriff
November 5   Alexandria Police Department Headquarters – 3600 Wheeler Avenue
- Alexandria Police Department
- Office of the Sheriff

Exhibit 2.2   Garner (North Carolina) 101 Presentation Schedule

Garner 101
Spring 2015
Class Format and Order of Presentations

Garner 101 will be conducted in a classroom setting where residents will learn about local government and the different roles each department plays in the overall function of the town. Classes will be conducted by department heads or designee and can include PowerPoint Presentations and/or field trips to public facilities where feasible. **Classes will be held from 6:30 PM – 8:30 PM unless otherwise noted.**

Order of Presentations

1.   Administration and Town Council; **Presentation date: March 5, 2015**; Town Hall Council Chamber; 900 Seventh Avenue, Building B.
2.   Public Information/Neighborhood Improvement and Raleigh Utilities; **Presentation date: March 12, 2015**; Dempsey Benton Water Treatment Plant; 2315 Benson Road, Garner, NC. Due to the length of the facility tour and the amount of information shared at this session, we will begin at 6:00 PM and conclude at 9:00 PM. Dinner will be provided.
3.   Inspections and Engineering; **Presentation date: March 19, 2015**; Senior Center, 205 E. Garner Road.
4.   Planning and GRA; **Presentation date: March 26, 2015**; Senior Center; 205 E. Garner Road.
5.   Public Works and All Star Waste; **Presentation date: April 9, 2015**; Public Works Administration Building, 610 Rand Mill Road.
6.   Finance and Chamber of Commerce; **Presentation date: April 16, 2015**; Chamber of Commerce, 401 Circle Drive.
7.   Police; **Presentation date: April 23, 2015**; White Deer Park Nature Center, 2400 Aversboro Road.
8.   Parks, Recreation and Cultural Resources; **Presentation date: April 30, 2015**; White Deer Park Nature Center, 2400 Aversboro Road. Due to the length of the facility tours and the amount of information shared at this session, we will begin at 6:00 PM and conclude at 9:00 PM. Dinner will be provided.
9.   Garner Fire and Rescue and Wake County EMS; **Presentation date: May 7, 2015**; 503 West Main Street.
10. Graduation: Community Leadership (School of Government) and introduction of all current Town Boards (Planning Commission, Parks Recreation and Cultural Resources Committee, and Senior Citizens Advisory Committee). **Graduation date: May 14, 2015**; Senior Center, 205 E. Garner Road. You are permitted to bring one quest.

*   **Attendance at seven (7) out of nine (9) sessions is required for graduation.**

On Your Own events

1.   Police ride-a-long
2.   Attend one Town Council Meeting prior to completion of Neighborhood College (mandatory)
3.   Attend one Parks, Recreation and Cultural Resources event **(at no charge to the student and a guest)**
4.   Download ***garner info*** app

Exhibit 2.3   Tamarac (Florida) University Class Schedule

CLASS OF 2016
CLASS
SCHEDULE

Welcome to the 2016 Class of Tamarac University. This 7-week interactive program will give you a behind the scenes look at Tamarac and the opportunity to meet your local government officials face-to-face. In a classroom-like atmosphere, you will learn from elected officials, department directors, and other City staff about the role of local government and public service. Additionally, Tamarac University serves as a training ground for volunteers in community service (including Tamarac's numerous Boards and Committees) and provides networking opportunities for civic-minded residents. Whatever your current role in our community may be, we encourage you to expand upon it and take part in building an even better Tamarac...
"The City for Your Life!"

Please note, order of presentations on any given evening is subject to change without notice. If you have questions or need directions to one of the locations where class will be held, please contact James Twigger at (954) 597-3904, or email tu@tamarac.org.

WEEK #1
Date: Tuesday, March 15, 2016
Location: City Hall
6:00 – Networking
6:30 – Opening Remarks
6:35 – Welcome from Mayor & Commission
6:45 – City Manager's Office
7:30 – BREAK
8:10 – Student Introductions
8:20 – Program Overview
• Rules and Decorum
• Hopes and Expectations
• Virtual Tour of Tamarac
• Pre-Test
9:00 - Class complete

WEEK #2
Date: Tuesday, March 22, 2016
Location: City Hall
6:00 – Networking
6:30 – Human Resources
7:00 – BREAK
7:20 – City Clerk's Office
8:00 – Class complete

WEEK #3
Date: Tuesday, March 29, 2016
Location:IT/Utilities Training Rm
6:00   Networking
6:30 – Information Technology
7:00 – BREAK
7:10 – Financial Services
9:00 – Class complete

WEEK #4
Date: Tuesday, April 5, 2016
Location: Fire Station 15
6:00 – Networking
6:30 – Fire Rescue
7:30 – BREAK
7:40 – Building
9:00 – Class complete

WEEK #5
Date: Tuesday, April 12, 2016
Location: BSO - Tamarac
6:00 – Networking
6:30 – Broward Sheriff's Office & Tour
7:30 – BREAK
9:00 – Class complete

WEEK #6
Date: Tuesday, April 19, 2016
Location: Recreation Center
6:00 – Networking
6:30 – Public Services
7:20 – BREAK
7:40 – Community Development
9:00 – Class complete

WEEK #7
Date: Tuesday, April 26, 2016
Location: Recreation Center
6:00   Networking
6:30 – Parks & Recreation
6:40 – Tour of City
9:00 – Class complete

WEEK #8 - GRADUATION
Date: Wednesday, May 11, 2016
Location: City Hall
6:00 – Program wrap-up
6:10 – Post-Test
7:00 – GRADUATION!

WWW.TAMARAC.ORG

Exhibit 2.4   Concord (North Carolina) 101 Session Sites Map

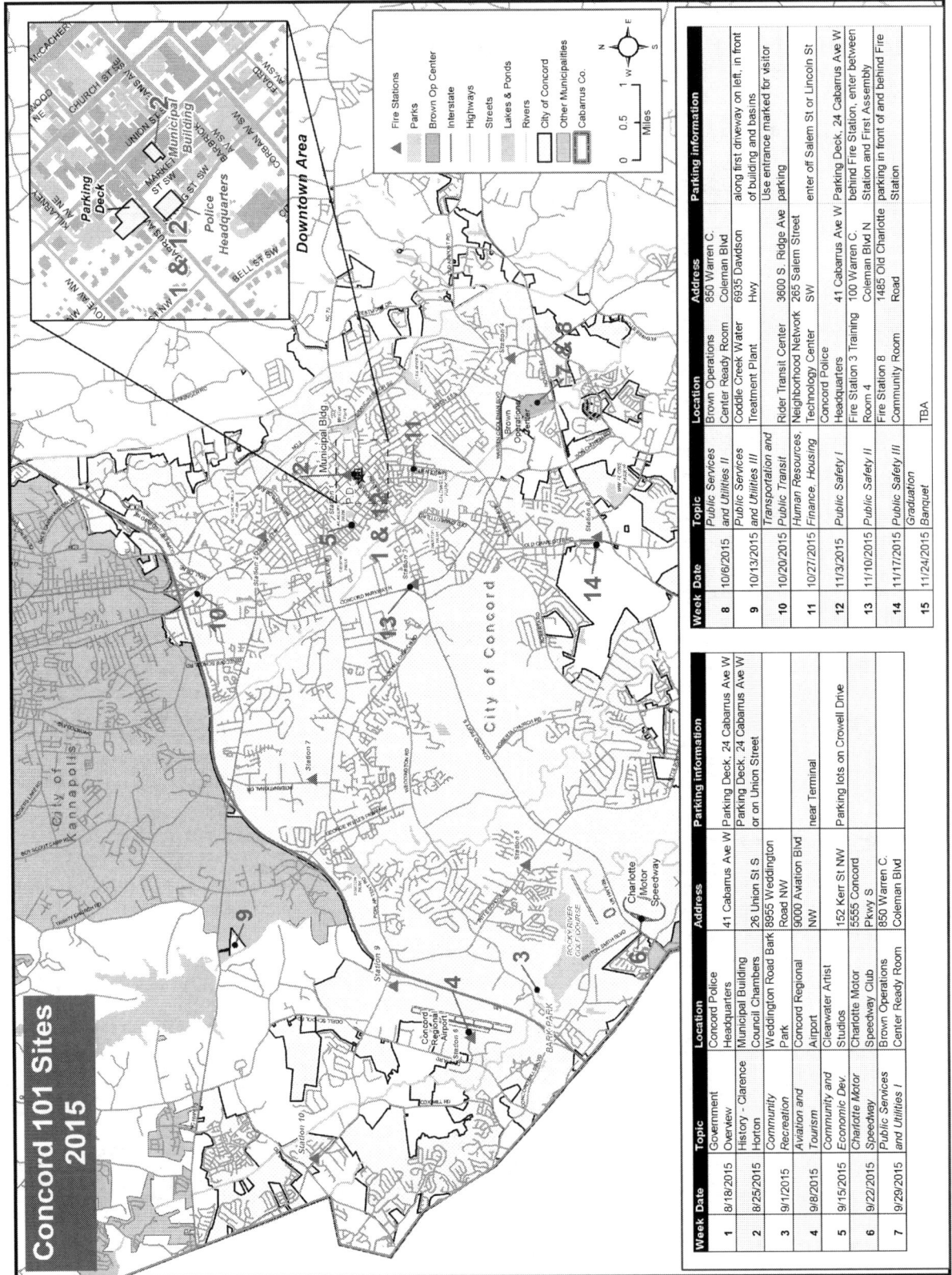

Concord 101 Sites 2015

Week	Date	Topic	Location	Address	Parking information
1	8/18/2015	Government Overview	Concord Police Headquarters	41 Cabarrus Ave W	Parking Deck: 24 Cabarrus Ave W
2	8/25/2015	History - Clarence Horton	Municipal Building Council Chambers	26 Union St S	Parking Deck: 24 Cabarrus Ave W or on Union Street
3	9/1/2015	Community Recreation	Weddington Road Park	8955 Weddington Road NW	
4	9/8/2015	Aviation and Tourism	Concord Regional Airport	9000 Aviation Blvd NW	near Terminal
5	9/15/2015	Community and Economic Dev.	Clearwater Artist Studios	152 Kerr St NW	Parking lots on Crowell Drive
6	9/22/2015	Charlotte Motor Speedway	Charlotte Motor Speedway Club	5555 Concord Pkwy S	
7	9/29/2015	Public Services and Utilities I	Brown Operations Center Ready Room	850 Warren C. Coleman Blvd	

Week	Date	Topic	Location	Address	Parking information
8	10/6/2015	Public Services and Utilities II	Brown Operations Center Ready Room	850 Warren C. Coleman Blvd	along first driveway on left, in front of building and basins
9	10/13/2015	Public Services and Utilities III	Coddle Creek Water Treatment Plant	6935 Dawdson Hwy	Use entrance marked for visitor parking
10	10/20/2015	Transportation and Public Transit	Rider Transit Center	3600 S. Ridge Ave SW	
11	10/27/2015	Human Resources, Finance, Housing	Neighborhood Network Technology Center	265 Salem Street SW	enter off Salem St or Lincoln St
12	11/3/2015	Public Safety I	Concord Police Headquarters	41 Cabarrus Ave W	Parking Deck: 24 Cabarrus Ave W
13	11/10/2015	Public Safety II	Fire Station 3 Training Room 4	100 Warren C. Coleman Blvd N	behind Fire Station, enter between Station and First Assembly
14	11/17/2015	Public Safety III	Fire Station 8 Community Room	1485 Old Charlotte Road	parking in front of and behind Fire Station
15	11/24/2015	Graduation Banquet	TBA		

Legend: Fire Stations, Parks, Brown Op Center, Interstate, Highways, Streets, Lakes & Ponds, Rivers, City of Concord, Other Municipalities, Cabarrus Co.

Miles: 0   0.5   1

Downtown Area

3. Who Is Going to Show Up?

> *I was so privileged to be asked to participate in this program which greatly broadened my knowledge of how our city government works. I am now able to share with other citizens just how "fine-tuned" our great city is!*
>
> **2012 Graduate of Winston-Salem (North Carolina) University**

Many established citizens academies are so popular that they are offered multiple times a year and always have a waiting list. Others, though, have been suspended due to (an apparent) lack of interest. Publicizing and recruiting participants is a key aspect of planning and executing a successful program. In these efforts it is important to find ways to get beyond the "usual suspects" so that citizens academy graduates are representative of the community as a whole.

In Chapter 1, we described how civic engagement is at the forefront of contemporary thinking and local government practice. The evolution of citizens academies has been a direct result of this emphasis as elected officials and administrators promote programs and policies that support citizen involvement in local governance. As mentioned in that earlier discussion, public administration scholars Jim Svara and Janet Denhardt have observed that "many local governments are examining ways to increase the opportunities for residents to be engaged in *informed* discussion with each other and with government officials."[1]

---

1. James H. Svara and Janet V. Denhardt, eds., "Connected Communities: Local Governments as a Partner in Citizen Engagement and Community Building," white paper (Phoenix, Ariz.: Alliance for Innovation, Oct. 15, 2010), 7 (emphasis added), http://icma.org/en/icma/knowledge_network/documents/kn/document/301763/

Informed is the key. As previously discussed, citizen engagement can be a useful tool for developing stronger, more beneficial relationships between citizens and government; however, people have to first possess the knowledge and perspective to engage meaningfully. While public officials have the benefit of being directly involved in policy matters day in and day out, the average person simply does not have the knowledge base to participate in those kinds of discussions in an in-depth way. Citizen academies, ideally, create collaborative learning environments in which attendees can develop that kind of understanding and perspective about the institutions and policies that govern and shape their communities.

But knowledge, while helpful, is itself not sufficient for effective citizen engagement. Citizens must also have a *willingness* to participate. Local governments may provide all kinds of opportunities for meaningful civic engagement, but that does not guarantee a productive process. To borrow from the classic film *Field of Dreams*, you can build it, but it is no sure thing that they will come. A local government can genuinely support deep engagement with its citizens, but that cannot become a reality unless members of the community are willing to give of their time and energy participating in civic affairs. That interest or willingness needs to be cultivated. Again, this is an important role citizens academies can play.

Diversity and Inclusion

In addition to ensuring that citizens are both sufficiently *informed* and *willing* to engage in local governance, striving for *diversity* and *inclusion* in terms of who "shows up" is another important part of the process. The National League of Cities (NLC) emphasizes the importance of inclusion in the following statement on civic engagement:

> NLC is contributing to a national effort to strengthen democracy and governance at the local level by involving residents in government and public life and by focusing on developing an *inclusive,* collaborative, and effective relationship built on trust between citizens and government. Through these relationships, communities can work together to arrive at solutions to pressing problems.[2]

connected_communities_local_governments_as_a_partner_in_citizen_engagement_and_community_building.

2. See the Civic Engagement page of the NLC website at www.nlc.org/find-city-solutions/city-solutions-and-applied-research/governance/civic-engagement (emphasis added; last accessed Aug. 23, 2016).

Participants in the Rockingham County (N.C.) Citizens Academy learning about the range of county functions that affect their day-to-day lives (Photo by Mabel Scott)

Building an environment that is "inclusive, collaborative, and effective" requires that the makeup of citizens academy classes go beyond what we might call the usual suspects, those residents who normally attend public meetings, who tend to be older, less racially and ethnically diverse, and more middle to upper income economically. Promoting diversity within programs might require exploring unique ways to actively recruit groups who historically have lived on the margins of a community.

Many, perhaps most, communities include certain members who traditionally have felt marginalized or unwelcome in the public spotlight. Engaging these groups can be especially challenging. In Oakland, California, distrust in government contributes to poor turnout for the city's Spanish-language citizens academy. The program manager continues to try new strategies to connect with this population, such as reaching out to stay-at-home moms by way of elementary schools and seeking funding for a program that would include ESL (English as a second language) classes via a partnership with the city library. But make no mistake; these barriers are difficult to overcome.

According to the Durham (North Carolina) Neighborhood College website, "applications will be accepted to create a diverse participant population from as many Durham neighborhoods as possible." Many programs include such language in their application materials. Some take a somewhat systematic approach to ensuring representation from all areas of the community by reserving a certain number of spaces from each ward or council district. Some even reserve a certain number of seats for youth or other special classes of individuals. Yet other programs report not needing to take special measures, as broad recruiting strategies bring in a diverse cohort every time.

Encouraging diversity can be as involved as running a separate, alternative-language program or as simple as reserving spaces for applicants from various areas of the community (by ward or council district, for example). The strategy for each program can, and should, reflect a community's particular circumstances and history. The main point here is that diversity needs to be consciously thought of, and program coordinators ought to develop a recruitment strategy that will make sure the program is inclusive and, to the extent possible, that participants reflect the diversity of the local community.

Recognizing and Removing "Invisible Walls"

An inclusive citizens academy program will actively recruit diverse participants and seek to ensure that a wide variety of backgrounds and viewpoints are represented and, more important, welcomed during each session. This kind of diversity not only creates a more dynamic learning environment, but it also helps the program benefit the entire community. Citizens academies can and should serve as a launching pad for citizen engagement that is inclusive and reflective of the community as a whole.

So what are some strategies that can help program organizers connect with those who often feel marginalized? In other words, how can a citizens academy be as inclusive and as welcoming to everyone as possible? One key is to avoid assumptions. In Chapter 2, within the context of thinking through logistical considerations, we introduced the idea of *invisible walls*. This term is found in Linda Stout's 1996 book *Bridging the Class Divide and Other Lessons for Grassroots Organizing*. According to Stout, those who work in a multiracial, multiclass environment need to keep in mind that everyone has a different way of communicating. Knowing where an audience comes from and how they will react to certain forms of speech and writing is key to building meaningful relationships that result in genuine outreach.

It's important that citizens academies seek out a diverse group of participants and recognize and remove the "invisible walls" that inhibit participation.

Administrators of a program that is intended to help produce a more knowledgeable and receptive citizenry must ensure that session materials, including the content and visuals used to market the program, are reviewed from the perspective of the different community populations who will view them prior to distribution. During program sessions, contributors must avoid bombarding participants with information that is too obscure or else risk turning them off to the entire educational experience. Any language barrier, whether between social classes or due to English as a second language, creates an invisible wall that must be scaled through conscientious planning at the outset of the program.

Another closely related assumption that program administrators should be careful to avoid relates to the existing knowledge of participants. For most attendees, day one of the citizens academy will be their first foray into local government and governance. For others, the course will be a refresher or add-on to their current responsibilities as public servants. Regardless, administrators will want to be very thoughtful about how they introduce the concept of a citizens academy to possible applicants and approach the lessons and key concepts that are addressed throughout the program sessions. It might be wise to start off by presenting the lessons at a beginner level and then to check in with the participants throughout the course to assess the feasibility of discussing the subject on a higher level. The last thing administrators should do is promote their citizens academy as a collaborative environment that welcomes people from all backgrounds only to have some of the participants feel excluded because the lessons cater more to some participants than to others.

Also, given that diversity is a necessary component of building a well-rounded, knowledgeable cadre of citizen thought leaders, those groups who consistently lack public representation at the decision-making table need to be considered. The next step is to figure out how to recruit and retain the interest of those individuals.

Thinking about Who Should Participate

Most programs prefer to cap enrollment at around 20 to 25 participants. A smaller class size permits more conversation during sessions and allows for more networking among participants and relationship building between citizens and staff. Some larger communities, including Buffalo, New York (population of 258,959), Fresno, California (population of 509,924), and Mecklenburg County, North Carolina (population of 990,977), extend their target participation total to 40 or even 50 participants. However, other larger jurisdictions, including Durham, North Carolina (population of 288,133), and Clearwater, Florida (population of 109,703), still aim for about 20 to 30 people, which appears to be the norm nationwide.

Many programs set the minimum age to participate at between 16 and 18, though in practice most programs are geared toward working adults and retirees. In a 2011 survey we conducted of graduates from 12 citizens academies, nearly 70 percent of respondents were 40 and older. As noted in Chapter 2, Martin County, Florida, attracts a large number of retirees and, thus, offers its program during regular business hours. Other program coordinators report having difficulty recruiting young to middle-aged adults for the usual 6 to 9 p.m. time frame due to family obligations.

Another frequently stipulated requirement is that applicants be residents of the community in which the program is being offered. In Durham, North Carolina, for example, program staff verify that applicants' property or vehicle taxes have been paid to the city or the county before they are accepted into the program. Kissimmee, Florida, meanwhile, uses an online pre-application residency verification tool. While some programs do not have a residency requirement (wanting to attract as many interested citizens as possible), this commonly applied rule is often expanded to include those who work for, or are owners of, a business within the community. Goodyear, Arizona, and Windsor, Connecticut, are two examples of programs that follow this practice.

Engaging Morrisville High School Students

The Town of Morrisville, North Carolina, successfully held its inaugural Teen Morrisville 101 session in spring 2015. The free program is geared toward ninth through twelfth graders interested in local government, whether they think they want to pursue a career in government or are just looking for greater insight into what it takes to run a town. The program provides participants with a behind-the-scenes look at how local government works, exposure to local government careers, and a chance to learn through a hands-on approach and group activities. Every session features a participatory portion to keep participants engaged and interested, for example, designing a park amenity and then presenting the plan at a mock town council meeting.

Recruitment

Town staff found that gaining entrée to the school system was challenging but were able to connect with a local high school principal who helped spread the word. Information on the program was also published in the monthly town newsletter, posted on the website and through social media channels, and advertised by the town council.

Logistics

While Teen Morrisville 101 program is open to all high school students, preference is given to local residents. To accommodate teen schedules, the program is held after school hours, on Thursdays from 3–5 p.m. for four weeks. It consists of four learning sessions plus an optional fifth, graduation session. The schedule is as follows:

- *Session 1*—Managing Information
- *Session 2*—Build a Park
- *Session 3*—Mock Town Council Meeting
- *Session 4*—Public Safety and You
- *Session 5* (optional)—Graduation

Some programs save spots for elected officials and staff. The Town of Pine Knoll Shores, North Carolina, hosted its first citizens academy in 2014. Over the course of its first two iterations, about 50 percent of participants were staff and elected officials. Similarly, program administrators in Martin County, Florida, encourage all elected officials and potential candidates to attend the Martin County CARES academy, and many do so. The inclusion of elected officials and candidates allows citizen participants to engage directly with their representatives. Attendance at their local government's citizens academy can even become part of the orientation process for newly elected officials.

Not surprisingly, the programs we have reviewed present various levels of participation by elected officials and staff. For instance, Ocean City University in Ocean City, Maryland, gives priority to property owners and residents but, if there is enough space, allows non-residents and staff to participate as well. Variation can also result from the form of government conducting the program. The Town of Lexington, Massachusetts, for example, has a representative town meeting form of government, and preference for admission to its citizens academy is given to those with fewer than five years of experience as town meeting members.

"Targeted" Participation

Catawba County, North Carolina, began offering its Government for Citizens program in 1994, with sessions running for two weeks on Tuesday and Thursday nights from 7 to 9 p.m. The program never gained traction, though, and was discontinued after a few years of weak attendance. After a number of years, county officials noted the need for greater civic education and engagement among particular pockets of the county and decided to offer a scaled-down version of the program solely for them. The idea was to engage specific citizens through a program that managed costs more efficiently. Today, Catawba County University is conducted for an estimated $300 per program.

The new program is offered directly to the targeted groups as well as to retirees on a Tuesday and Thursday over the course of a single week. The course has been offered in the fall and runs from 10 a.m. to 3 p.m. or occasionally 3 to 6 p.m. The public information officer (PIO), who coordinates the program, organizes regular sessions on the council–manager form of government, the county budget, public safety, social services, and public health. Because the class roster is decided about a month in advance, and participants are asked beforehand what they would like to learn about, the PIO is able to design a final session based on those choices (e.g., economic development, green/environmental initiatives, etc.).

2014 graduates of Winston-Salem (N.C.) University (Photo by City of Winston-Salem)

The targeted participation model has been the modus operandi ever since the county received feedback that citizens find it hard to participate in a program held at night over the course of several weeks. Shortly after switching to this new model, the county was asked to create a modified version for leaders of the local Hispanic community. "This group meets monthly on Monday nights and wanted us to present portions of our academy on selected Monday nights across many months," Catawba County Public Information Officer Dave Hardin said. To start, participants of the Hispanic leadership academy learn about the organizational structure of the county before moving on to sessions about the basic operational functions of its government, including a session on budgeting and a session on public health and social services.

It is critically important to think carefully about who the ideal participants are so that it is possible to create a program that meets the needs of those audiences. Bend (Oregon) 101 uses the tagline "Give us five hours and we'll give you the City" to project its flexibility in offering citizens an educational experience that fits their busy schedules. It even offers interested organizations the option to build their own citizens academy experience based on the particular topics they are most interested in learning about. This customizable format allows Bend to offer its program for free and deliver its citizens exactly what they are looking for.

But even beyond meeting citizens' needs, the program must also be marketed in such a way as to attract those target audiences. Going directly to them, as Catawba County does, is one way to approach it. Adapting program delivery to meet their specific needs is another approach that communities like Bend are trying.

Alternative Language Programs

There are many examples from across the country of municipalities that are striving to introduce quality civic education to non-English-speaking populations. In Oakland, California, for example, where nearly 17 percent of the population is Asian-American and more than 25 percent are Hispanic or Latino, the city has sought to provide for both communities in its program planning. Instead of offering separate programs, some communities hire an interpreter to be present at their English-language program. In addition, the City of Clearwater, Florida, provides American Sign Language translation for their deaf attendees.

Creating a Recruitment and Advertising Plan

Most communities recruit applicants to their programs using unpaid advertising tools, such as the following:

- fliers at local government facilities (examples are presented in Appendix 3);
- city/county print and electronic newspapers or newsletters;
- city/county website;
- press releases, which sometimes lead to newspaper articles and radio announcements (examples are presented in Appendix 3);
- utility billing inserts;
- local government cable television access programming;
- staff visits to neighborhood associations, civic clubs, and the like;
- chamber of commerce newsletter or visit;

Spotlight on Oakland, California

The Oakland Citizens' Academy takes place annually in late summer/early fall and has been run out of the city's Equal Access Office since 2005. The program offers concurrent sessions in Cantonese and Spanish in addition to the English-speaking program.

"The Chinese academy has an active alumni organization that meets regularly and participates in a lot of civic engagements," reports Silvia San Miguel, program manager for the Citizen Academy. "The whole point of the Citizen's Academies is to let people know how the city works and where to go in case they have a problem. Once they have that information it gives them the knowledge and confidence to get what they need. If a resident doesn't speak English they can call us and we will get them an interpreter to help them communicate with whatever city department can help them."

Just as in the English-speaking sessions, Cantonese and Spanish participants meet with representatives from every department in the city and with most department directors, thereby receiving high-level access to city leaders. San Miguel noted less success enrolling Spanish-speaking as compared to Cantonese-speaking participants due to the Spanish-speaking population's underlying distrust of government. However, she is constantly reevaluating her strategies geared toward connecting with this segment of the population.

Note: This sidebar is drawn from Institute for Local Government, "City of Oakland's Citizen Academy," www.ca-ilg.org/public-engagement-case-story/city-oaklands-citizen-academy (last accessed Aug. 23, 2016).

- posts on Facebook, Twitter, and other social media sites; and, perhaps *most important,*
- word of mouth by alumni and/or staff and elected officials.

Some organizations have opted to supplement their unpaid methods with paid advertisements, including

- newspaper, radio, and television ads and
- Internet advertising (such as ads on Facebook).

While word of mouth is still far and away the most important and successful publicity tool, organizers should consider also using public advertising, especially in the inaugural year. In the first year of its citizens academy, for example, Hillsborough, North Carolina, relied on newspaper ads but in subsequent years added word-of-mouth "advertising" from alumni, which resulted in a noticeable boost of applicants. In Cherryville, North Carolina, staff members and elected officials have approached citizens directly, giving them an extra nudge to attend. This is more feasible in smaller communities, but larger programs also report wide success with invitation-oriented approaches. Working through churches, schools, neighborhood and other community organizations (places where community members already gather) can be an effective way to reach beyond the usual suspects. (See Figure 3.1.)

As noted above, word of mouth is reported by program coordinators as the best method of advertising. The reason is simple: when someone you know and trust recommends something to you, that carries much more weight than generic advertising, whether a notice included in utility bills or a message that shows up on a Facebook newsfeed. Obviously the best way to create positive word of mouth is to have a citizens academy that is memorable, engaging, and worth the participants' time. Those who have a good experience are likely to share that with friends and acquaintances. However, do not take word of mouth advertising for granted. Devoting a few minutes of the final session to encouraging participants to invite friends to apply can make a difference. Better yet, send them home with fliers to share with friends, neighbors, or fellow congregants. Or, when the next application cycle begins, email or message your alumni and ask them to spread the word in person and through social media. The power of word of mouth simply cannot be overstated.

> *Thank you for the time, energy, and commitment you have for this class. I have already told 10 people about it.*
>
> Decatur 101 Participant

Figure 3.1   Variety of Means Used to Recruit Participants

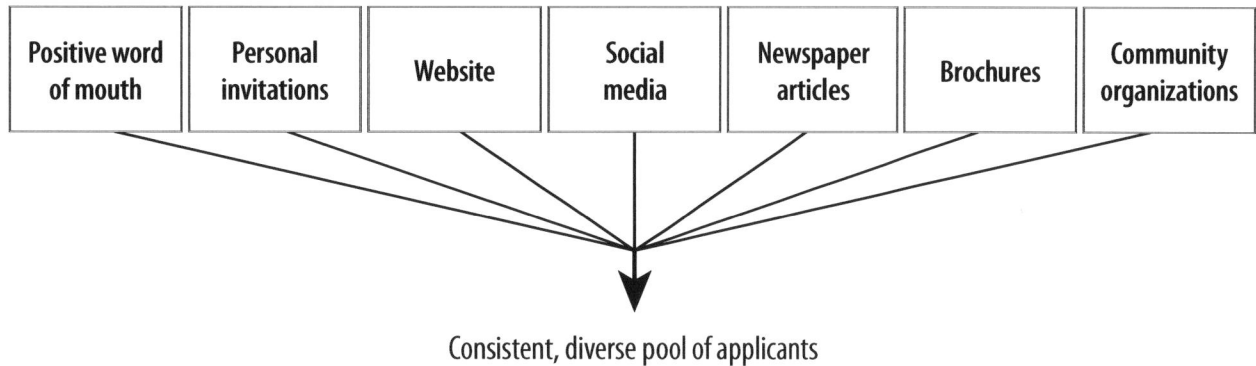

| Positive word of mouth | Personal invitations | Website | Social media | Newspaper articles | Brochures | Community organizations |

Consistent, diverse pool of applicants

If resources are available, it might be worthwhile to create a separate brand identity for the citizens academy to help distinguish it from other programs and services the organization may offer. For instance, a logo and tagline with distinctive design and colors could be easily incorporated into any of the above mentioned advertising methods to help shape people's perception of the program as a legitimate source for civic capacity building within the local community.

Selecting Participants

Waiting lists might need to be used regardless of how participants are chosen, and there are two primary ways by which cities and counties select applicants to their programs.

First-come, first-served is the most commonly used application/selection process nationwide and is perceived to be most fair. Volusia County, Florida, for instance, uses this method but has altered it slightly. The interests of those applying are considered: the participants chosen under first-come, first-served must meet with a county staff member before final acceptance to explain their interest in participating.

A smaller number of cities and counties opt instead to *hand pick applicants to obtain a diverse cross-section* from their communities. Usually, this includes diversity in the following respects:

- residency (including how long applicant has resided there
  or if applicant only works in the community),

Citizens Academy
Cultivating Tomorrow's Civic Leaders Today

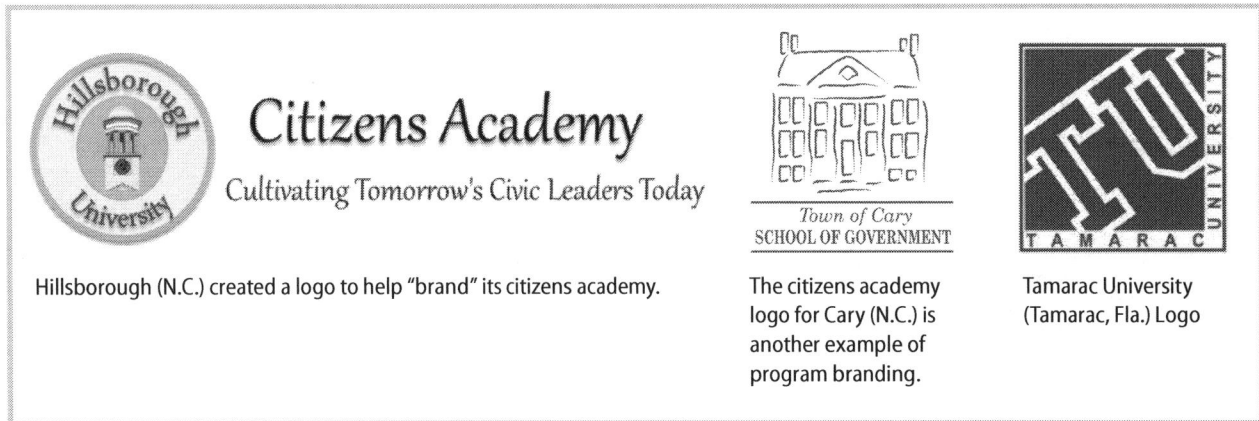

Hillsborough (N.C.) created a logo to help "brand" its citizens academy.

Town of Cary
SCHOOL OF GOVERNMENT

The citizens academy logo for Cary (N.C.) is another example of program branding.

Tamarac University (Tamarac, Fla.) Logo

- neighborhood representation,
- age,
- gender, and/or
- race and ethnicity.

Larger cities like Greensboro and Durham, North Carolina, use this method. The small town of Two Rivers, Wisconsin, does as well and has its program organizing committee (consisting of staff from the finance, fire, and police departments, among others) review applications. Usually, one staff member reviews the applications and decides who is selected, or a committee of staff members is charged with selecting the participants. As noted before, some programs have an advisory committee or board of some kind made up of alumni, and such bodies can also be employed to select participants.

Until 2010, Cherryville, North Carolina (mentioned above, with a population of around 6,000), had staff and council members brainstorm in selecting a cross-section of residents to attend the program. After that, staff reached out and asked citizens to participate. Currently, though a new application system solicits more applicants, staff still look for representation from a cross-section of the community in terms of age, gender, and neighborhood locations.

Other variations on the selection process include that of Moore County, North Carolina, where newly elected officials, appointed board members, and new residents are given first priority. Greenville, North Carolina, gives first priority to elected officials representing the city's five council districts (five spots). The remaining slots are reserved for residents, with any slots left over given to residents of the city's extraterritorial jurisdiction.

Delray Beach, Florida, Moore County, North Carolina, and Morrisville, North Carolina, are examples of communities that offer separate programs for high school–aged youth, who can garner hands-on civic education and even earn service hours for their participation. These communities also explicitly encourage staff participation in their program, as does Kannapolis, North Carolina, where the program directed toward the educational advancement of staff is held during lunch hours, separate from the sessions for city residents.

Most cities and counties notify all applicants of their participation status through letter or e-mail. Accepted applicants are asked to rsvp and usually commit to attending every session. Notification has been reported as an essential step, especially if there is a waiting list.

Waiting Lists

The number of applicants sometimes exceeds the target number of participants and usually does in well-established programs. Some communities facing this issue use a waiting list, while others simply suggest to those citizens who are not chosen that they apply again for a future program. Waiting lists are very common. Usually the number is small, a dozen or less. There are exceptions, however, such as Martin County, Florida, Buffalo, New York, and Fresno, California, all of which report having more than 100 people waiting for slots to come open. This will undoubtedly remain the case until more sessions are offered, especially for larger jurisdictions with popular programs.

Clearwater, Florida, and Durham, North Carolina, both of which accept between 20 and 30 participants in each program, take alternates from their waiting lists if anyone in the first round of selected participants drops out after only one or two sessions. This ensures that citizens who are truly interested in the program will have a chance to participate. Waiting lists can also serve as a recruitment tool; those left on the waiting list from one year are often given preference for the following session. This allows for a constant stream of participants when there is steady interest in the academy.

Drafting the Application

Citizens academy applications vary widely in the information they request from potential participants. Short applications tend to focus on verifying residency (e.g., Durham, North Carolina). Some require applicants to explain their interest in wanting to become involved in the community (e.g., Greensboro, North Carolina,

Engaging High School Juniors in Chula Vista

The City of Chula Vista, California, Citizen's Youth Leadership Academy offers a behind-the-scenes look at city government to a very specific group of individuals in the community—eleventh graders. Over the course of six sessions, the high school juniors attend informative presentations and participate in tours of facilities around town. Participants also have the opportunity to interact with elected officials, department heads, and frontline staff. For instance, one highlight of the program is a Saturday morning bus tour with the mayor. Other sessions include lessons on police and fire safety, conservation, city finance, planning, recreation, road improvements and library services.

The program encourages students to become better informed as future community leaders. It is also a tool to encourage students to finish high school. Mayor Cheryl Cox stated in an informational letter directed at applicants in 2014 that "it will highlight career opportunities available to students who graduate from high school and will help you understand the necessary training and education needed for jobs in public service and other sectors as you make plans for your senior year, graduation, career training and/or college. In short, graduation works!"†

Class sessions are scheduled for weekday evenings (when school is not in session) and a study hall is offered directly beforehand, followed by a complimentary dinner. The students receive twenty hours of community service credit upon successful completion of the program.

† Undated letter from the Office of Mayor Cheryl Cox, www.chulavistaca.gov. See also League of California Cities, "California City Solutions: Chula Vista's Youth Leadership Academy Opens Eyes of High School Students to City Government," www.cacities.org/Top/News/News-Articles/2015/June/California-City-Solutions-Chula-Vista-s-Youth-Lead (last accessed August 23, 2016).

and Chula Vista, California). Others require applicants to list the organizations and activities in which they are involved to support their case for seeking further involvement in the future. Examples of citizens academy applications are included in Appendix 3.

When crafting the application, it is again important to try to avoid putting up "invisible walls" to potential participants. For example, questions should be reviewed for being potentially intimidating or exclusionary. Request information that is necessary for the selection process used, whether first-come, first-served or one based on criteria applied to achieve a diverse cross-section of attendees. Also, the application process should be *easy*. Most application processes continue to be paper-based, but the ease of creating webforms (even with something as basic as Google Forms) is such that there is no reason not to make applying online an option.

The application and selection process need not be complicated, but it is important to consider inclusiveness and diversity throughout. The same is true for program marketing. Utilizing word of mouth is critically important. And the myriad of free ways to get the word out—whether social media or an organization's website—also should be fully utilized. But we also recommend extending special invitations to certain persons or groups. A citizens academy that is as diverse as the community it serves will, in the long run, do more for the community in terms of capacity building than a program that, while popular, is made up mostly of the "usual suspects."

Questions to Consider

What kinds of people are you looking to attract as participants in the program?

_____

_____

Is it important for you to have a diverse representation of the community in the program, or are you looking to reach out to a specific group of residents?

_____

_____

How are you structuring the program so that it is convenient and welcoming to the target audience you are looking to attract?

_____

_____

What are some creative ways that you can take advantage of resources already available in the community to advertise the program?

_____

_____

How can you fully leverage positive word of mouth?

_____

_____

How can you create tools/avenues for advertising the program that will reach your target audience?

_____

_____

How will you select participants should you have more applicants than seats available? If you have a waiting list, what will it mean to be on the waiting list?

_____

_____

How can you make the application easy to find, fill out, and elicit the necessary information for the selection process?

_____

_____

Appendix 3   Exhibit Items

Exhibit 3.1   Ocean City (Maryland) University Brochure

Week 13 - People, Safety and Insurance

Participants learn about Ocean City's Risk Management Department, safety and self-insurance programs. The Human Resources Department discusses labor and employment issues.

Week 14 - The Waterworks – History and Development of the Water and Wastewater Departments

Participants learn how the Water and Wastewater Departments operate. Class includes a tour of both facilities, including the new bio-solids plant.

Week 15 – Fun in the Sun

Students learn about the Ocean City Convention Center and its role in promoting tourism. An overview of public relations is also provided.

Ocean City University is sponsored by the Mayor and City Council of Ocean City, Maryland. Registration and classes are free.

For More Information Contact:
Diana Chavis, City Clerk
Jessica Waters, Communications Manager
P.O. Box 158
Ocean City, MD 21843
410-289-8842
dchavis@oceancitymd.gov
jwaters@oceancitymd.gov

OCEAN CITY UNIVERSITY

❋ This is a 15-course program. Classes are once a week for 8 weeks in the fall and 7 weeks in the spring. Each class is two hours long. One class hour equals one credit. Students can earn a total of 30 credits, which will earn them a Bachelor's Degree in Municipal Citizenship

❋ A Master's Degree in Municipal Citizenship can be obtained by completing the Citizen's Police Academy for an additional 33 credits.

❋ A Doctorate Degree in Municipal Citizenship can be earned by completing the Community Emergency Response Team (CERT) program.

**Ocean City University
Founder:
Kathleen A. P. Mathias
1953 - 2011**

OCEAN CITY UNIVERSITY

TOWN OF OCEAN CITY SPONSORED CIVIC EDUCATION PROGRAM FOR OCEAN CITY RESIDENTS

ESTABLISHED 2004

Exhibit 3.1   Ocean City (Maryland) University Brochure (*continued*)

OCEAN CITY UNIVERSITY

❋ Ocean City University was developed to provide public education and information on government services, public policy, organizational structure and operations. The curriculum covers all facets of municipal government.

❋ Students enrolled in Ocean City University have a better understanding of the government's role and relationship with its citizens and gives them a sense of ownership in government actions.

❋ Citizens and government work together to improve the quality of life for Ocean City residents. These informed citizens make a difference in the community.

COURSE OFFERINGS

Week 1 - Freshmen Orientation, History of Ocean City & Government Overview

Offers an introduction to municipal government. Students learn about the council-manager form of government, organizational structure of departments and intergovernmental relationships. Volunteerism on town boards is discussed. An overview of the OC Life-Saving Station Museum is included.

Week 2 - Finance 101

Students learn about the budget and budget process, how their tax dollars work and gain an understanding of the financial operations of Ocean City.

Week 3 - Trains, Planes and Automobiles

Learn about the operation of the town's municipal bus system and how it relates to traffic in Ocean City. Course also covers the municipal airport and includes a tour of the facility.

Week 4 - Keeping the Records and Following the Law

Studies the inner workings and duties of the City Clerk's office. The City Solicitor will provide an overview of his position and role in government. The Chief of Police will give an overview of the police department.

Week 5 - What Makes the City Run

Course looks at the town's purchasing processes, procedures and fleet management. Students learn about Information Technology and what's behind the scenes making everything work. Program includes a tour of the service center and warehouse.

Week 6 - Emergency Services

Studies in this program include a look at Communications, Emergency Management and Radio Communications. Participants also tour the communications center.

Week 7 - When you Call 911, 911 Calls Us

A look at our fire responders, fire protection services and emergency medical services from 3 divisions of the Fire Department.

Week 8 – REC 101 Studies in Recreation and Sports

Course provides an overview of recreation programs and services. Students learn about all recreation operations including Eagle's Landing Golf Course, Ocean City Tennis Center and Special Events Programs

Week 9 - Planning and Community Development 101

Course covers general duties and responsibilities of Planning and Community Development, including GIS and zoning overview.

Week 10 - Construction and Permits

Students learn about the permit process for building and construction. How the department works and the role of the building inspectors are just some of the topics covered.

Week 11 - Engineering and Environmental Services

Curriculum covers operations of the Engineering Department and duties of the City Engineer. Included is engineering's role in protecting the environment of the Maryland Coastal Bays.

Week 12 - Behind the Scenes – Public Works Operations

Course covers the operations of the Public Works Department from Administration to Maintenance, Construction and Solid Waste.

Exhibit 3.2   Application to the 2016 Clearwater (Florida) Citizens Academy

CITIZENS ACADEMY

LEARN ABOUT
GOVERNMENT
FROM THE
INSIDE OUT

Clearwater Citizens Academy focuses on educating residents about local government processes. Elected officials, department directors and other city staff will host unique and informative sessions designed to give residents a hands-on experience in city government operations.

Take the class. Be informed and involved. Join other residents who help keep our community strong by actively participating in city affairs.

10-SESSION CURRICULUM
Application Deadline: Aug. 1, 2016
Orientation is Tuesday, Sept. 6, 2016, 6 to 8:30 p.m.
Other classes are Tuesday evenings, beginning Sept. 13, 2016, 6 to 8:30 p.m.

APPLY NOW!
APPLICATION ON BACK

Sponsored by the city of Clearwater Public Communications Department

Exhibit 3.2   Application to the 2016 Clearwater (Florida) Citizens Academy (*continued*)

CITIZENS ACADEMY
CLASS APPLICATION, Fall 2016
(Please attach additional pages as needed)

Name:				
Mailing Address:				
City:		State: FL	Zip:	
Home Phone:		Business Phone:		
E-Mail Address:				

	Yes	No
I am a resident of the incorporated city of Clearwater	Yes	No
I am a business owner in the incorporated city of Clearwater	Yes	No

Tell us a little about yourself (past employment, organizations in which you are, or have been active, and special interests):

Please tell us why you would like to participate in Clearwater 101:

What do you consider your major strengths and qualifications for Clearwater 101?:

How will our community benefit from your participation in Clearwater 101?:

Shirt Size:	☐ Male ☐ Female	S	M	L	XL	2XL

ALL SHIRTS ARE PRE-SHRUNK COTTON

Do you or have you served on a city board in Clearwater? If so, which one?:

How did you hear about the Citizens Academy?:

Applicant Personal Commitment
If selected I will devote the time necessary to meet graduation requirements. If chosen, I will attend at least eight (8) of the ten (10) sessions. I will continue to stay involved in city government to the best of my ability and act as an ambassador by sharing my knowledge with other Clearwater citizens.

Applicant's Signature: _____ **Date:** _____

Please send or fax your completed application to:	For the safety of participants, a background check will be completed on all applicants. For that purpose, please include the following:
Public Communications Department **City of Clearwater** **P.O. Box 4748** **Clearwater, FL 33758** Fax: (727) 562-4696 *Questions? Call (727) 562-4708*	**Race** _____ **Gender** _____ **Date of Birth**

Exhibit 3.3   City Press Release on the Clearwater (Florida) Citizens Academy

City of Clearwater

Public Communications, Post Office Box 4748, Clearwater, Florida 33758-4748
100 South Myrtle Avenue, Clearwater, Florida 33756
Telephone (727) 562-4284   Fax (727) 562-4696

For Immediate Release
July 10, 2015

Contact:
Heather Parsons
(727) 562-4708
Heather.Parsons@myclearwater.com

Learn About Government from the Inside Out

CLEARWATER, Fla. -- Applications are now being accepted for the fourteenth year of Citizens Academy, Clearwater 101, a ten-week program providing citizens with a hands-on learning experience about the people, equipment and infrastructure it takes to run Pinellas County's second-largest city. The program will begin with orientation on Tuesday, Sept. 8 from 6 to 8:30 p.m. The classes that follow will also be on Tuesday evenings from 6 to 8:30 p.m. through graduation on Nov. 18.

This interactive program is an educational experience for Clearwater residents interested in city affairs. Sessions are led by elected officials, department directors and city staff who share information about the city's operations and key issues facing Clearwater today. Participants must attend at least eight of the ten sessions in order to graduate at the City Council meeting on Wednesday, Nov. 18.

A selection committee will choose 20 participants from the applications received. The committee will judge applications based on responses to questions while ensuring that the class reflects the diversity of the Clearwater community, with representatives from different neighborhoods and sections of the city. Applications are available online at myclearwater.com or http://bit.ly/1pkgkGC, or residents can call (727) 562-4708. Applications must be received no later than Monday, Aug. 3.

# # #

George N. Cretekos, Mayor

Bill Jonson, Councilmember   Jay Polglaze, Councilmember
Hoyt Hamilton, Councilmember   Doreen Hock-DiPolito, Councilmember

"Equal Employment and Affirmative Action Employer"

Exhibit 3.4   Application to Concord (North Carolina) 101

Office Use only:

Date received: _____

Concord
NORTH CAROLINA
High Performance Living

Concord 101 Application Form

Due August 2, 2014
Email: franzese@concordnc.gov
Mail: P.O. Box 308, Concord, NC 28026

Name (First, MI, Last): _____

Mailing Address: _____

Reside in City Limits: (circle one) YES or NO

Zip Code: _____

Phone: _____-_____-_____

E-mail address: _____

How long have you resided in Concord? : _____

Occupation: _____

Educational Background: _____

Why are you interested in Concord 101? _____
_____
_____
_____

Other past or present community activities: _____
_____
_____
_____

Past City government service or involvement (such as serving on a board), if any: _____
_____
_____
_____

Are you available for weekly Tuesday meetings from 6:00 p.m.-9:00 p.m. (circle one)? YES or NO

☐ **Please check the box to verify that you are 18 years of age or older. Class size is limited, and preference is given to City of Concord residents.**

Notice: The City of Concord does not discriminate on the basis of age, sex, race, religion, national origin, or disabilities. If anyone needs special accommodations, please contact Peter Franzese at franzese@concordnc.gov. This application may be available in an alternate format for users with special needs.

Exhibit 3.5   Application to Greensboro (North Carolina) City Academy

City Academy

City Academy is a unique opportunity for residents to learn about City of Greensboro government in order to promote a better understanding and working relationship between the two. One of the program's components is to prepare students for service on a City board or commission. The City Academy is not open to City employees. To be considered for the 2014 session, fill out this application and return it to the address below by July 15. For more information on City Academy, call 373-2723.

GREENSBORO

Full Name _____ Nickname _____

Mailing Address _____ Zip _____

Phone #   Home _____   Work _____   Cell _____

Email _____

Employer Name & Address _____

Birth date _____   Shirt Size   Men's _____   Ladies' _____

If accepted to the 2014 City Academy do you agree to share the above information with your classmates and City staff for contact purposes only?

☐ Yes I agree   ☐ No please do not share

Are you currently a member of any City of Greensboro Board or Commission: If yes, which ones?

☐ Yes   ☐ No

Board or Commission	Title or Role	Dates

Please list all civic, professional, business, religious, social or other organizations of which you are a member or on which you have served. If you are new to Greensboro, you may include activities in your prior location.

	Organization	Years as Member	Position Held
Please answer all fields if applicable			

Anyone who submits a form should be aware that in accordance with the North Carolina Public Records law, found in NCGS Chapter 132, his or her information submitted is considered public record.

Exhibit 3.5   Application to Greensboro (North Carolina) City Academy (*continued*)

Briefly discuss what you hope to learn as a participant in the City Academy and how you plan to use the information.

_____

_____

_____

How did you hear about the City Academy?

_____

_____

The City Academy regular sessions will be held primarily on Thursday evenings (exceptions noted below) from 5:45 – 9:00pm from September 4 through November 18. Will you be able to attend all classes? If no, please describe:

☐ Yes   ☐ No _____

#	DATE OF SESSION		NAME OF CLASS
1	September 4, 2014		**Ready, Set GOv!**
2	September 11, 2014		**Roads, Recycling & Rights of Way**
3a	September 18, 2014		**To Serve …**
3b	September 20, 2014	*SATURDAY*	**Inside the Perimeter** *(elective session)*
3c	September 23, 2014	*TUESDAY*	**… And Protect** *(elective session)*
4	October 2, 2014		**Whatever Moves You**
5	October 9, 2014		**Rescue Me!**
6	October 16, 2014		**Plan On It/Neighborhood Development**
7	October 23, 2014		**At Your Leisure/Water At Your Service**
8	October 28, 2014	*TUESDAY*	**A World of Possibilities/ Human Relations**
9	October 30, 2014		**Boards & Commissions/$how Me the Money**
10	November 6, 2014		**First Point of Contact**
11	November 13, 2014		**Are You Smarter Than A CSR/ Boards and Commissions**
12	November 18, 2014	*TUESDAY*	**Graduation**

The City Academy will be held at various locations throughout the City. Would this create a transportation issue for you? If yes, please describe

☐ Yes _____   ☐ No

How long have you been a Greensboro resident?   _____

The City of Greensboro is committed to inclusiveness and diversity. In order to help us achieve this goal, please answer the following questions (optional):

2

(*continued*)

Exhibit 3.5   Application to Greensboro (North Carolina) City Academy (*continued*)

Gender: ☐ Male ☐ Female   Race: [   ]   Ethnic Background: [   ]

Please describe what is unique about yourself.

_____

_____

_____

_____

What are your expectations related to City Academy?

_____

_____

_____

_____

Do you need any special accommodations? If yes, please describe   ☐ Yes   ☐ No

_____

Do you have any special food requirements or limitations? If yes, please describe ☐ Yes   ☐ No

_____

Are you willing to serve on a Board or Commission?
        ☐ Yes   ☐ No

The Greensboro Police Department performs a background check on each City Academy applicant. A felony conviction automatically excludes an applicant from participating.

        ☐   *By checking the box, you have agreed to the disclaimer.*

Return this form to: Community Relations   Telephone: 373-2723
                        City of Greensboro   Fax: 373-4656
                        P.O. Box 3136   E-mail: communityrelations@greensboro-nc.gov
                        Greensboro, NC 27402

3

4. Making the Content Interesting and Engaging

> *It wasn't just a classroom setting. It was very hands-on. The guest speakers were knowledgeable and entertaining and spoke on a variety of interesting topics. They kept us very engaged.*
>
> Montgomery County–Christiansburg Citizens Academy alum

Now that the strategies for attracting a diverse, motivated group of community participants has been discussed, the next step is to figure out how best to keep those individuals interested and engaged during the program itself. Let's face it: *local government administration* doesn't exactly scream "exciting!" And yet, local government provides the backbone, the infrastructure, of community itself. Most of the key elements of "quality of life" either directly come from, or are directly impacted by, the workings of local government. The challenge is determining how to present content in a way that speaks to the audience, engages them, and even at times inspires them.

Principles of Adult Learning

Staff involved with citizens academies should think about how to convey content in ways that increase the likelihood that attendees will be glad they came and so that lessons learned will stick in their minds long after the last session. A great place to start is by considering some proven principles for connecting with adults in the classroom. Consider the following quote from the book *Active Training* (2006) by

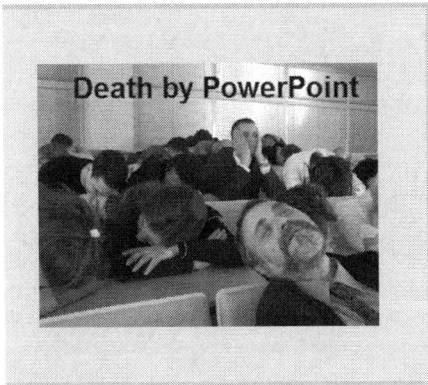

It doesn't have to be this way.

Mel Silberman, professor emeritus at Temple University and a pioneer in the field of educational psychology and training:

> Learning cannot occur simply by listening and seeing. It requires the person's own mental processing to take place. Therefore, lecturing by itself will never lead to real learning.[1]

Although presenting information about many local government departments is conducive to PowerPoint, and a lecture-style mode of delivery is usually acceptable in such settings, if the goal is to impart actual knowledge and, moreover, to engender genuine engagement, sessions need to move above and beyond the use of PowerPoint.

Active Learning

The best lessons are structured to reinforce active learning and adult-learning principles, both of which center on the notion of the instructor (staff) teaching *with* learners (citizen participants) rather than *at* them. In *Active Training*, Silberman discusses the need for messaging to be conveyed in multiple modes of delivery in order to appeal to students' various learning styles. For instance, auditory learners tend to be most comfortable with lecture-style presentations, visual learners prefer actual demonstrations of concepts, and kinesthetic learners process information best through hands-on activities. Regardless of the specific learning type, however, there are proven benefits of going with a more active learning approach, namely, that

1. audience attention wanes less quickly;
2. it appeals to the majority of learning styles, not just to auditory learners; and
3. it promotes higher level retention of factual information.

Having at least a cursory understanding of active learning principles is thus very helpful in designing and conducting a successful citizens academy.

Silberman's model of active learning outlines six systems or modes of delivery to be aware of when structuring lesson plans. *Incorporating two or more of these principles into a lesson plan dramatically improves the ability of program*

---

1. Melvin L. Silberman, *Active Training: A Handbook of Techniques, Designs, Case Examples, and Tips*, 3rd ed. (San Francisco: Pfeiffer, 2006), 71.

Mel Silberman's "Active Learning Credo" (adapted from a well-known Confucian proverb)

- When I only *hear*, I forget.
- When I *hear* and *see*, I remember a little.
- When I *hear*, *see*, and *ask questions*, and *discuss* with someone else, I begin to understand.
- When I *hear*, *see*, *question*, *discuss*, and *do*, I acquire knowledge and skill.
- When I *teach* someone, I master what I have learned.

Source: Melvin L. Silberman, *Active Training: A Handbook of Techniques, Designs, Case Examples, and Tips*, 3rd ed. (San Francisco: Pfeiffer, 2006), 2.

participants to walk away having actually processed the information rather than simply having heard it and possibly retained it in the short run. The six delivery systems/modes are (1) hearing, (2) seeing, (3) questioning, (4) discussing, (5) doing, and (6) (learner-based) teaching.

To demonstrate the significance of both *hearing* and *seeing* a lesson versus just hearing it, consider that the inclusion of visuals in a lecture can improve audience retention 14 to 38 percent.[2] Furthermore, when vocabulary is taught using visual aids, retention is improved up to 200 percent.[3] This is because the brain uses a visual-only format to store information. Examples of visual learning at a citizens academy might be a local paramedic demonstrating how to give CPR on a dummy, distributing hard copies of a PowerPoint presentation before presenting, or using a slideshow of images to assist a lecture.

Creating an environment that encourages *questions* can take learning to a whole other level. Questions not only elicit interest and engagement; their use also creates a more collaborative learning environment, making the conversation go two ways rather than just one. Questions can help presenters hone in on aspects of the content that are most meaningful to participants as well as lead to discussions. Sometimes an activity as simple as passing out notecards or sticky notes before the

---

2. Robert W. Pike, *Creative Training Techniques Handbook: Tips, Tactics, and How-To's for Delivering Effective Training*, 3rd ed. (Amherst, Mass.: HRD Press, 2002), 63, https://books.google.com/books?id=aUY7cVz8f3oC.

3. Pike, *Creative Training Techniques Handbook*, 63.

Presenting tip: A nice way to kick off presentations in an engaging way is to begin with a mini-quiz, audience poll, or questions for the audience. This method not only helps pique the interest of participants (to answer the questions correctly), but it can also help the presenter gauge the knowledge level of the audience and subsequently adapt the presentation to their needs and interests.

presentation begins and asking participants to jot down one or two questions they have about the topic can help jump-start a session and make it more interactive.

A key aspect of active learning is creating opportunities for participants to *discuss* the information they've been given. Blocking off time for peers to hold conversations among themselves following a presentation gives them time to develop their own understanding of the concepts and to visualize them being used in real-life situations, which also helps with retention. In fact, it is recommended that individuals be given a chance to internalize new content (in some way) *every eight minutes*[4] throughout a presentation. Sticking to similar intervals of discussion time among peers could promote better retention of key principles and also foster a collaborative environment in which program attendees feel encouraged to participate in class.

At the heart of Silberman's active learning model is the ability of participants to *do* something with the knowledge they've just acquired. This might take the form of a mock debate, with each half of the classroom arguing one side of a pertinent issue currently being considered by the city council. It could involve a budget game through which participants have to evaluate trade-offs similar to what their elected officials face during the budget process. It could include a scavenger hunt that sends participants around city hall or across town or a requirement that they sign up for a police ride-along before a session on public safety. The value of incorporating an active learning system of delivery into a lesson plan that requires direct application of information that previously was an abstract concept cannot be overstated.

Information that participants retain, digest, and actively apply to real-life situations can be strengthened further still by their synthesizing the information and *teaching* it to others. For the same reason that discussing an idea is better than simply hearing and seeing it applied, being able to teach a concept is considered the

---

4. Pike, *Creative Training Techniques Handbook*, 34.

Presenting tip: It is important for presenters to remember that "less is more." Fewer slides, less text on slides, and less speaking by the presenter allows for more questions, more discussion, and more time to experience hands-on learning.

highest level of learning because it requires knowing enough about the subject to be able to explain it concisely and coherently to others. One way to allow participants the opportunity to apply their knowledge in this fashion would be to have individuals prepare their own presentations on relevant subject matter and share them with the class. Or, better yet, assign homework whereby participants teach what they have learned to a friend, neighbor, family member, and so on. These can be great ways to make the content both matter and stick with participants.

Although people may personally prefer one mode of learning over another, combining various systems of delivery in presenting content increases the likelihood that the lessons will resonate with as many individuals as possible. Take care to not overdo it, though. Depending on the age, temperament, individual attention spans, and learning styles of participants in a particular session, cramming too much activity into the lessons could be viewed as tiring, even bothersome. The key is to settle on a variety of active learning approaches that best align with the individual learning styles present in each citizens academy class. To get a sense of how incoming program participants learn best, staff could consider sending a brief poll or assessment to gain a baseline sense of which activities will appeal to the new class.

Collaborative Learning Environments

Ideally, citizens academies should be environments where participants feel supported, especially by their peers, on their journey toward increasing their knowledge of local government. This collaborative setting should encourage a thoughtful exploration of relevant subjects and lead participants to learn both *with* each other and *from* each other. In order for this to occur, staff need to be aware that the quality of engagement and connections among program participants have a direct effect on how well they learn.

Research has shown that people need to feel safe and secure in a social environment before they can be empowered to engage in the types of active learning principles necessary for greater knowledge retention. Icebreakers, group activities, and other social events held prior to and throughout program sessions can be an essential investment in program success. Thus, having a meal as part of each session has benefits well beyond simply providing an incentive to come. Breaking bread together can be a great way for participants (and staff) to get to know one another, which will help create a comfortable and therefore better learning environment.

Jerome Bruner's *Toward a Theory of Instruction* (1966) uses the word "reciprocity" to describe the deep need people have to bond in order to work together toward a common objective. This human tendency supports the need for citizens academies to encourage and support a diverse exchange of ideas as well as allow individuals to collaborate in working toward the common goal of preserving and improving their communities.

Creating collaborative learning environments thus yields benefits in addition to improved learning. Citizens academy alumni often comment on the social networking aspect of their experience. Getting to know others in their community, as well as local government staff members, expands their social networks. Social scientists call this "bridging" social capital. People's normal (and by-and-large homogenous) social circles (family, work, church) are called "bonding social capital," which of course is important in terms of individual well-being and support. But it is bridging social capital that establishes linkages *across* an individual's social circles, and across the community, offering important community and societal benefits.

Communities with more bridging social capital are more prosperous and resilient. Communities with a rich stock of bridging social capital are more adept at working together to solve problems and move forward.[5] Thus, in designing citizens academies with an eye toward collaborative learning, organizers must remember that *learning is only one goal.* Creating new relationships and strengthening the social infrastructure of the community is another, perhaps higher level, goal.

Creative Ways to Present Content

Citizens academies can be (and perhaps often are) taught in a thorough, monotonous fashion featuring much lecturing and PowerPoint presentations with the occasional stretch break. Unfortunately, such presentations tend to support the

---

5. The seminal work on social capital is Robert Putnam's classic study *Bowling Alone: The Collapse and Revival of American Community* (New York: Simon & Schuster, 2000). Much research on the topic has followed, but Putnam's book is a great place to start to better understand the concept. See also the About Social Capital page of the Harvard Kennedy School website, www.hks.harvard.edu/programs/saguaro/about-social-capital.

long-standing stereotype of the bureaucrat droning on, speaking bureaucratese, to an un-engaged audience. But it doesn't have to be this way. The programs that are very popular, that generate a lot of positive word of mouth from alums, *truly engage and inspire participants.*

Part of the secret is simply finding staff members that want to (and can) teach, that have a passion for their topic and are excited to share information about what they do with an interested audience. These people are there, in every organization, and they often make great teachers. The other part of the equation is devising creative methods for teaching and involving participants in fun lesson plans and learning formats.

To keep participants engaged in the topic at hand, department presenters can be encouraged to go beyond PowerPoint by making their presentations interactive and engaging. Below we review five categories of creative content presentation especially relevant to citizens academies. They are:

1. experiential learning activities,
2. field trips/tours,
3. homework,
4. games, and
5. mutual learning.

1. Experiential Learning Activities

Experiential learning activities engage citizens directly. In the view of education scholar Peter Jarvis, experiential learning is about learning through the senses.[6] While participants can learn through staff presentations and lectures, lessons that are taught "first-hand" to allow participants to physically and mentally engage in the learning process, through demonstration, participation, and individual action. MIT professors David Kolb and Ronald Fry's model of experiential learning emphasizes the need for (1) concrete experience, (2) observation and experience, (3) the formation of abstract concepts, and then (4) testing in

> *Our tours of our city's water treatment facilities were very interesting. We the public take our water for granted. The other day I saw someone (not a city employee) who had opened a fire hydrant, so I called the local police department and reported it. That is something I would not have done prior to the classes. Also, if I am ever asked to serve on [a] committee, such as parks and recreation, I would do so. Prior to the classes I would not have been willing to serve.*
>
> 2011 Graduate of the Cherryville (North Carolina) Citizens Academy

---

6. Peter Jarvis, *Adult and Continuing Education: Theory and Practice*, 2nd ed. (London: Routledge, 1995).

Greensboro (N.C.) City Academy participants operating a fire hose with the Greensboro Fire Department. Hands-on activities are not only fun, they are proven to be more engaging and memorable for participants.

new situations.[7] While learning can begin at any of the four points, experiential learning is best approached as a continual cycle.

Experiential learning can be demonstrative. One example would be having a local police department show off the practicing commands of their K-9s. Another example can be having the local fire department showcase firefighters arriving at a scene and using the Jaws of Life to rescue a trapped person, as is done during one session of the City of Hickory, North Carolina, citizens academy.

Experiential activities can also be participative, such as the fire department allowing participants to hold and operate a fire hose. Some programs even include the opportunity to fire weapons at the firing range—always a very popular activity in programs that do this.

---

7. David A. Kolb and Ronald Fry, "Towards an Applied Theory of Experiential Learning," chapter 3 of *Theories of Group Processes*, edited by Cary L. Cooper (London: Wiley, 1975).

Participants in Decatur (Georgia) 101 get to play the roles of developers, noisy neighbors, or the planning commission during a mock meeting. Another creative way that Decatur gets participants to learn about their town in an interactive manner is by sending them on a scavenger hunt geared toward informing them about local places of interest (see questions for the 2015 scavenger hunt in Appendix 4). The activity requires participants to visit various public buildings and other landmarks around the city and answer such questions as, "There is a bust of Commodore Stephen Decatur on the marta [Metropolitan Atlanta Rapid Transit Authority] plaza area. Who donated the bust to the City of Decatur?" Another question asks, "Fire Station #2 is located at 356 W. Hill Street and has received a LEED [Leadership in Energy and Environmental Design] Silver certification. Visit the Fire Station, find the Big Red 2 and name one other component that helped make it LEED certified."

In addition, experiential learning can also take a more independent form. For instance, citizens may be asked to take pictures of their favorite offerings within the community and discuss their photo choices in groups. Some programs send participants on self-guided tours as a homework assignment. Given the ubiquity of smartphones, asking participants to take and upload pictures of favorite places, or problem areas, or images that represent issues they care about can be an easy, experiential add-on to a program. Some programs now have Facebook and Instagram pages that can facilitate this kind of experiential (and collaborative) learning through social media technology that most people use every day.

The Redwood City (California) PACT program (Partnership Academy for Community Teamwork) strives to make every session engaging. The first half-hour of each session is dedicated to participants eating together and sharing stories. The remaining hour-and-a-half is devoted to the session topic, which always focuses on (and is held at) a different city facility.[8]

Ideas for participant icebreakers and innovative topic formats abound. Some include

- game show– or board game–type quizzes (e.g., on city/county history),
- behind-the-scenes tours of facilities (e.g., the public works operations center/city garage),

> *I enjoyed doing the scavenger hunt, budget activity and smart growth tour, Decatur history. . . . This was a great program and I really enjoyed it.*
>
> 2011 Graduate of Decatur 101

---

8. See Ed Everett, "Community Building: How to Do It, Why It Matters." *ICMA IQ Report* 41, no. 4 (2009): 1–14.

- demonstrations of equipment (e.g., fire trucks),
- informal interactions with city/county staff (e.g., dinner with elected officials or city/county employees),
- group exercises and simulations (e.g., a mock council meeting where budget decisions must be made),
- attendance at a local government board meeting,
- scheduling a police ride-along,
- participating in a community service project or effort, such as a community garden.

As part of Decatur 101, participants take part in a brainstorming activity in which they consider how to coordinate across different departments in order to solve the issue: "Where can the Book Festival place a Cooking Stage?" They also have an activity called "build your neighborhood" using pictures from magazines.

2. Field Trips/Tours

Successful programs often include field trips and tours. These creative teaching activities can be done as a group, such as touring a golf course during a session on parks and recreational offerings, or as an individual assignment, such as scheduling a ride-along with law enforcement. Such field trips and tours can be chiefly informative, experiential, or both.

For instance, in order to graduate from Winston-Salem (North Carolina) University, students must tour a city facility outside of regular class time. They can choose to shadow a City Link (call center) agent for one hour, explore the Recreation and Parks rock quarry when it was being developed as a public park, tour the local wastewater treatment plant or the contracted recycling center. Participants are required to complete one tour but can schedule as many as their curiosity and schedules allow. Likewise, participants of the Buffalo, New York, citizens academy must go on a police ride-along or take a complaint call in the Mayor's Call and Resolution Center.

Tours can also be self-led, as in Winston-Salem, where participants must ride a city bus before graduating from the academy. Many programs ask participants to attend a meeting of the community's elected board (examples include Lauderdale Lakes, Florida, and Rockingham County, North Carolina). Similarly, Garner, North Carolina, showcases its Parks, Recreation, and Cultural Resources department by providing students with free passes to different program offerings. Participants can opt to experience the municipal performing arts center, visit Lake Benson and rent a paddleboat for a day, or enjoy a free pool pass, among other options.

The Town of Cary (N.C.) School of Government makes sure that each session includes an exercise and a tour or other non-lecture activity. Experiential learning is thus built into the agenda.

Session 1: Introduction
Ask participants to identify themselves and share how they found out about the course or why they applied; then hold a short reception with council members.

Session 2: Planning
Divide participants into groups and create an area plan that meets defined parameters.

Session 3: Development Process
Have participants review simplified site-plan submittals and critique plans based on provided criteria.

Session 4: Budget and Finance
Give groups a list of capital projects and costs and ask them to decide which projects to fund with a given amount of cash and debt (be sure to include the question of whether or not they are willing to raise taxes).

Session 5: Municipal Services—Utilities
Organize a bus tour of the water system cycle (start at the intake pump station, stop at the water treatment plant and water tank, pass by the sewer pump station, and end with a tour of the wastewater plant).

Session 6: Municipal Services—Public Works
Offer a tour of the operations center and equipment demonstrations (showing how a hydrant works, salt/sand domes and loaders, in-pipe cameras, a sewer jet truck, a trash truck, etc.) and allow participants to operate the trash truck joystick to pick up the cart and empty it into the truck.

Session 7: Municipal Services—Public Safety
Provide firefighting and rescue demonstrations followed by an Emergency Response Team (SWAT) demo, K-9 demo, and an opportunity to shoot at the range.

Touring a water treatment plant in Cary, North Carolina (Photo by Bruce Rosar)

Following are several tips for coordinating tours of local departments and facilities:

- Let the departments define the best date and time for a tour by working with the facility manager to determine a schedule of dates and times when students are allowed to participate.
- It is more convenient for participants to have various time and date options. Having at least one weekend tour option is helpful.
- Follow up with the facility manager to confirm participation.

Self-Tour Ideas
Participants may enjoy experiencing the community on their own time. Here are some suggested self-tour ideas for students to undertake.

- Ride the local transit system to work one day.
- Take a nature walk at a community park.

- Tour utility facilities (water, wastewater, electric) to see how basic services are provided behind the scenes.
- Enjoy a day at the recreational facility (lake, pool, theater, etc.); be sure to offer passes for family members as well.

3. Homework

While some programs emphasize their lack of homework and tests, others embrace assignments as helpful learning tools. When tied to learning outcomes of the program, homework assignments can provide review opportunities and helpful clarification to participants. They also can be used to engage participants outside of the citizens academy program. As mentioned in Chapter 2, Garner, North Carolina, strongly encourages participants to complete out-of-class homework in the form of exploring the town on their own time. These activities include going on a police ride-along, attending a Parks, Recreation, and Cultural Resources event, or downloading the free Garner Info mobile app.

As noted above, the City of Decatur, Georgia, assigns a homework scavenger hunt (see Appendix 4) that is due on the first session. This assignment requires participants to visit several sites in order to answer questions relating to the city and city services. The assignment is intended to allow participants to visit places they may not have seen or known about prior to the program. It is also fun and can be accomplished with families or groups of friends.

The City of Raleigh, North Carolina, requires participants to complete two homework write-ups and a final case study assignment. The two homework write-ups are due at separate times, and both are reactions and reflections to municipal meetings (city council or citizen advisory boards). The final assignment is intended to encourage participants to think about solving a community problem in their neighborhood. This project allows participants to use their newly acquired knowledge and apply it to an improvement plan that can be acted on beyond the program.

Rockingham County, North Carolina, also requires participants to complete homework to review lessons learned in the sessions. While very few programs give traditional homework assignments, participants of the Cary, North Carolina, citizens academy are required to do some advance reading. As part of the Kannapolis (North Carolina) Citizens Academy, participants are asked to complete, prior to the planning session, a homework assignment of taking photos of their community. Concord, North Carolina, on the other hand, explicitly advertises its program as not requiring homework but offers an optional scavenger hunt activity for participants.

Excerpt from Decatur 101 Scavenger Hunt

Please answer the questions and/or fill in the blanks by visiting the sites described. Bring your completed form to the first session of Decatur 101.

1. There is a bust of Commodore Stephen Decatur on the marta plaza area. Who donated the bust to the City of Decatur?

2. There are three Decatur leaders mentioned on plaques on and around the square in downtown Decatur. They are located on a structure, a statue, and a plaza. Who are the three leaders and what is named for each?

3. Stop by the Decatur Visitors Center, 113 Clairemont Ave., and discover something that you did not know (preferably about Decatur). What did you learn?

4. The old section of the Decatur Cemetery is now listed on the National Register. There is a plaque located at the Commerce Drive entrance (near the Well House) describing the cemetery. Based on the information on that plaque, how many acres does the cemetery comprise and how many grave sites does the cemetery contain?

5. Visit Glenlake Park and find the adult playground equipment. Try it out and describe your experience.

4. Games

Games are an entertaining, accessible way to engage participants. Many programs use the familiar game show styles of *Jeopardy, Who Wants to Be a Millionaire?* and *Family Feud* to showcase unfamiliar information. Templates for such game formats are easy to find online. For example, Winston-Salem University uses a Jeopardy-type game to help participants solidify what they have learned. At the end of the ten-week program, participants play the game to test their knowledge of each department's presentations. As a staff member reported, playing games "helps them think about how the information can be used to help other citizens when confronted with issues." To spur friendly competition, the winning team gets a prize, such as posters left over from a centennial event the year before.

Even more technical topics, such as budgeting and finance, can be made to be engaging. Clearwater 101 presents information about city finances through a game show–like role-playing activity that uses participants as contestants. Similarly,

Permits	Geography	Volunteers - Employees	Land Use	Potpourri
100	100	100	100	100
200	200	200	200	200
300	300	300	300	300
400	400	400	400	400
500	500	500	500	500

This body issues a Certificate of Appropriateness for exterior work within a historic district

Stills from the Jeopardy game used at Winston-Salem (N.C.) University

Winston-Salem University participants are required to participate in a budget project over the course of about three weeks. In small groups of four or five, participants are presented with a budget and approximately ten line items. Together, groups must choose five items to cut. On graduation night, each group presents their budget findings and recommendations. By participating in their own budget exercise, students gain a greater understanding of and appreciation for difficult budget decisions faced by the council and staff (see Exhibit 4.2 in Appendix 4).

The Decatur 101 program includes a budget game that has participants use 100 pennies in a "How would you spend your tax dollar?" exercise. Participants are divided into small groups of no more than eight participants and given 100 pennies to represent one tax dollar. First, they must count out 68 pennies and set them aside; these go directly to the school system. This leaves 32 pennies to cover all city services. (The penny budget exercise is among the exhibit items included in Appendix 4.)

A game developed by the UNC School of Government (SOG) called Budgetopolis is a thorough, yet fun and effective, way to teach students about municipal budgeting (a county version of the game is called Bottom Line). Played in small groups that simulate elected boards, the game requires participants to begin by agreeing on what they value most about their municipality or county. In rounds that present real-world budget challenges, such as a natural disaster or state-mandated cut, players are given alternatives for cutting services and options to generate revenue. Participants are asked to balance the budget while considering the long-term impact on their communities. A facilitator from the School of Government can help program organizers think through how the simulation will be most effective in their particular jurisdiction or group and will even bring the game to you.[9]

5. Mutual or Collaborative Learning

Citizens academy participants can be valuable community members, as academy sessions provide the foundation for deeper citizen engagement to connect and collaborate. As John Peters and Joseph Armstrong explain, "Collaboration means that people labor together in order to construct something that did not exist before the collaboration, something that does not and cannot fully exist in the lives of individual collaborators."[10] Collaborative learning requires the joint contribution

9. For more information, go to the Budget Simulation page of the SOG website, www.sog.unc.edu/resources/tools/budget-simulation.

10. John M. Peters and Joseph L. Armstrong. "Collaborative Learning: People Laboring Together to Construct Knowledge." *New Directions for Adult and Continuing Education* no. 79 (Fall 1998): 75.

Participants play the UNC School of Government's Budgetopolis game

not only of participants, but of program staff who are willing to forgo a top-down teaching method in order to come to more inclusive solutions.

In citizens academies, sessions are most successful when they are designed to provide opportunities for mutual learning and networking. As noted earlier, each session is a chance to build social capital. Peters and Armstrong note that traditional teacher-student roles can undermine mutual learning opportunities, even outside the traditional classroom. If the staff presenter is viewed like a traditional teacher, and participants view themselves only in the role of student, opportunities for collaborative learning may be missed. Peters and Armstrong argue that, instead, presenters can, by relinquishing some of their power, encourage the students to assume greater responsibility for what happens as a part of the teaching-learning experience. In a collaborative citizens academy setting, coordinators and presenters should avoid presenting themselves as the sole experts or the only decision-makers. Instead, they should take on the role of the facilitator, encouraging collaboration and building social capital.

Spotlight on the Raleigh Neighborhood College

The Raleigh Neighborhood College was reporting middle-of-the-road evaluation scores for the statement: "The sessions are providing opportunity to engage with classmates." The coordinator wanted to do something to enhance participation by the 25 participants in each session, so he searched for ways to create more mutual learning opportunities. "Only 30 percent of the presentations [give participants a chance to] work out a problem together or go on a field trip, which offers small group communication and opportunities to have physical, hands-on experiences." Recognizing this, the program began instituting icebreaker questions twice each class session—once at the beginning of class and once upon the return from break.

One of the program coordinator's favorite icebreaker questions is: *What is your favorite childhood toy?* "You can learn so much about a person that way. . . . What generation they come from, how big their family is, to the participants' personality types! Most people want you to hear their stories, where they came from, why they have the opinion they do, and this communication can be much richer and jam-packed with insight when you feel 'safe and comfortable' with the participants you are sharing the experience with."

These types of icebreaker questions also bring about unexpected bonuses: "the instructor becomes more relaxed, and the presentation becomes more personable, due to the short term connection they have allowed themselves to be a part of."

At the end of the first session, the program coordinator chooses two students and asks each of them to choose an icebreaker to begin the following session. This responsibility rotates among all participants and continues as a light (and often lighthearted) way to ease into each session.

The Raleigh (North Carolina) Neighborhood College, like many other programs, aims to build social capital by having participants eat dinner together before class starts. The program provides a comfortable space, as well as the food, and participants automatically start to interact, thereby building bonds that will enhance engagement.

To sum up, interactive exercises, such as tours, games, and budgeting simulations, create fun and exciting learning opportunities that allow participants to view local government from a new perspective. This change in perspective can build confidence and encourage participants to pursue advisory board and volunteer positions. Collaboration during the learning experience is the adhesive that causes the lessons and experiential learning activities to stick, and resonate, in people's minds. A one-way, top-down learning experience is not going to be as effective as allowing the flow and exchange of ideas to come from the group as a whole.

Choosing the Right Presenters and Coordinators

It is important that presenters at any given citizens academy session be knowledgeable, engaging, and enthusiastic. Longtime Cary (North Carolina) School of Government program coordinator Lana Hygh shares her perspective: "It is very important to choose great presenters. Department directors are usually best because of their broad knowledge, but it is also important that they be dynamic presenters and very positive about their profession, the organization and the community."

While dynamic department directors are easily the best suited for delivering informational department overviews, tours and demonstrations may best be led by ground-level staff. The Town of Cary uses this strategy successfully. Hygh notes that "we also use 'line' employees for the public works sessions (especially demonstrating equipment, etc.). They take great pride in showing what they do to serve Cary citizens and this comes through in their demonstrations and explanations; they are always well received by participants."

Because the goal of a successful citizens academy is ultimately to spur civic engagement and public trust among participants, choosing a program coordinator/manager who is passionate about local government and the community is an absolute must. This person needs not only to be knowledgeable about the town's various departments and programs, but also to have the ability to work with key contacts from other areas and carry out the agenda items for each lesson in an upbeat, inspiring manner.

Choosing a Presenter Checklist

Is the staff presenter
- broadly knowledgeable on the session topic area?
- an engaging and dynamic presenter?
- enthusiastic about their job and profession?
- positive about the organization?
- community-minded?

A stellar citizens academy coordinator/manager will be

1. *Passionate*—This person's passion and dedication to public service need to be palpable; mannerisms and enthusiasm for various aspects of local government set the stage for citizens to imagine the roles that they might start to play in improving their own communities.
2. *Knowledgeable*—This person knows the ins and outs of local government or at least has insider access to resources that will be useful to pull from while teaching lessons throughout the duration of the program.
3. *Connected*—This person needs to be able to collaborate with cross-departmental and community partners to achieve program objectives. This may mean that the manager has already established relationships with department directors who might be open to hosting an experiential learning activity at their facility.
4. *Creative*—This person is aware that the best types of learning experiences go beyond PowerPoint and tirelessly explores ways to keep participants engaged, whether through scavenger hunts and other group activities, guest speakers, and facility tours.
5. *Approachable*—This person understands that he or she is the face of government and that the success of the program depends on the participants feeling they are part of a positive, collaborative learning environment.
6. *Flexible*—This person is eager for feedback and is constantly looking for ways to improve the program.

Getting to be a part of the experience of fostering better informed citizens can be a rewarding experience. However, the nature of how lessons are presented can make or break the success of citizens academies because so much of the material is funneled through the perspective of a single program manager. Whether the staff member delivering the content is the city manager, public information officer, or an intern, he or she should serve as a helpful resource and a living example of citizen engagement.

Regardless of whether an elected official, city manager, or other upper-level administrator ends up serving as the program manager or a guest presenter, his or her involvement (however large or small) is vital to the success and continuity of a citizens academy. As mentioned in Chapter 1, there must be support from upper management and elected officials to ensure that at least one person at the decision making table can speak to the program's merits as a tool for civic capacity building.

Finally, citizens academy oversight is moving innovatively toward a collaborative model that engages past participants in design, planning, and evaluation. Here a coordinator works with an advisory board or committee of past participants to oversee the program. This model may be more time-intensive for staff, but in terms of building social capital—of leveraging the citizens academy to build civic infrastructure within the community—it may be the best vehicle to take toward realizing those goals. The usefulness of this model will be discussed further in subsequent chapters.

Questions to Consider

Based on the time allotted for each session, would a demonstrative or participative approach be more appropriate when incorporating experiential learning activities into the curriculum?

_____

_____

Does the class seem to be more comfortable working on activities in groups or independently?

_____

_____

Which sites around your city would be interesting and relevant destinations for a field trip to learn about the various topics covered in the curriculum?

_____

_____

Are you accommodating any limitations (i.e., physical, mental, financial, etc.) that might deter people from participating in activities that are more interactive?

_____

_____

Does the space where classes are to be conducted have the audio-visual capability to show PowerPoint images, videos, and other graphic representations included in your lesson plan?

_____

_____

What icebreakers or other fun activities can you facilitate at the beginning of and throughout the sessions to help participants get to know one another?

_____

_____

Who from the department has the right combination of time, energy, and knowledge about the inner workings of local government to present the citizens academy curriculum in a dynamic and engaging format?

_____

_____

Appendix 4   Exhibit Items

Exhibit 4.1   Decatur (Georgia) 101 Scavenger Hunt 2015

Decatur 101 Scavenger Hunt

Please answer the questions and/or fill in the blanks by visiting the sites described. Bring your completed form to the first session of Decatur 101.

1. There is a bust of Commodore Stephen Decatur on the MARTA plaza area. Who donated the bust to the City of Decatur?

2. There are three Decatur leaders mentioned on plaques on and around the square in downtown Decatur. They are located on a structure, a statue, and a plaza. Who are the three leaders and what is named for each?

3.   Stop by the Decatur Visitors Center, 113 Clairemont Ave. and discover something that you did not know (preferably about Decatur). What did you learn?

4. The old section of the Decatur Cemetery is now listed on the National Register. There is a plaque located at the Commerce Drive entrance (near the Well House) describing the cemetery. Based on the information on that plaque, how many acres does the cemetery comprise and how many grave sites does the cemetery contain?

5. Visit Glenlake Park and find the adult playground equipment. Try it out and describe your experience.

6. At the intersection of Lucerne, Geneva & Champlain (in the Great Lakes neighborhood) there is a marker designating Gladys Morgan Waddell Park. On the stone marker is a quote. What is the quote and who is the author? Who gave the Park to the City of Decatur and when was it dedicated?

Exhibit 4.1   Decatur (Georgia) 101 Scavenger Hunt 2015 (*continued*)

7. Decatur has a thriving Oakhurst business district located at the intersection of Oakview and East Lake Road. Visit one of the stores or restaurants and bring a menu or a card from the establishment with your completed form. What establishment did you visit and what type of business is it?

8. The Oakhurst Community Garden is located on Oakview (as you turn the corner from S. McDonough). Visit the garden and find the bench next to the pond. Take a minute to sit down on the bench and look at the garden. What is your favorite thing in the garden? Describe it or draw it here:

9. Who is the sculptor of the "Valentine" and "Thomas Jefferson" statues located in front of the Old Courthouse on the Square?

10. Columbia Theological Seminary is located on Columbia Drive. Find the 12-foot Celtic Cross on their campus. Where is it? Who gave it to the seminary?

11. Fire Station #2 is located at 356 W. Hill Street and has received a LEED Silver certification. Visit the Fire Station, find the Big Red 2 and name one other component that helped make it LEED certified.

12. There is a boulder in front of the Decatur Recreation Center. Who does it describe and why is it there?

13. Visit one of Decatur's Dog Parks. Where is it? What is unique about it?

Exhibit 4.2   2013 Winston-Salem University Budget Exercise

BUDGET EXERCISE
March 21, 2013

- The FY 13-14 budget is balanced, and the City Council will consider the budget for adoption in a matter of days.

- The City Council has already incorporated the following measures to balance the budget without a property tax rate increase:
    - No increase in employee pay for the coming year
    - No increases in service levels
    - Limited replacement of vehicles and equipment
    - No change in support to community agencies

- As part of the State's tax reform efforts, the General Assembly has passed legislation that will eliminate the City's local business privilege tax, for a loss of $2.4 million in FY 13-14.

- It is an election year, and a majority of the Council Members has pledged not to increase the property tax rate. (1¢ = $1.9 million)

- Staff has been directed to put together a list of options for re-balancing the budget.

- As Council Members, your role is to choose 5 of the following 10 options to bring the budget back into balance. The savings amount does not reflect actual service cost reductions. The savings are provided to focus attention on service impacts, rather than the real savings that might be associated with each option.

Proposed Budget Reduction Options	Savings
1. Change code enforcement (e.g., minimum housing, weeded lot, sanitation, abandoned vehicles) from systematic and complaint-based inspections to complaint-based only.	$480,000
2. Eliminate bulky item collection service, which is currently provided to all residents, once a year.	$480,000
3. Eliminate 12 firefighter positions previously funded by a grant, which would reduce "extra coverage" citywide to help maintain an average response time of 4 minutes or less.	$480,000
4. Reduce the vegetation management program scope, resulting in fewer tree replacements, less litter pick-up on the right-of-ways, reduced mowing frequency along major and minor streets (including US 52 and Business 40), and replacement	$480,000

Exhibit 4.2 2013 Winston-Salem University Budget Exercise (*continued*)

of landscaping of medians with wood chips, etc.	
5 Reduce the number of special units in the Police Department, such as the gang unit.	$480,000
6. Reduce the leaf collection service by providing 2 rather than 3 seasonal pick-ups per household.	$480,000
7. Close 3 of 8 swimming pools, based on utilization, and convert 2 from pools to spraygrounds.	$480,000
8. Decrease the frequency of transit service for the public bus system and on-call service for the elderly and disabled.	$480,000
9. Reduce programming in the Recreation and Parks Department, resulting in reduced hours at the City's 17 recreation centers and elimination of the adult softball program.	$480,000
10. Reduce support for arts and sciences community agencies. *(Budget includes $195,000 for the Arts Council, $170,630 for SciWorks, $48,750 for Old Salem, $73,130 for National Black Theatre Festival, $36,570 for RiverRun Film Festival, and $25,000 for the Piedmont Triad Film Commission.)*	$480,000

Exhibit 4.3   100-Penny Exercise for Decatur 101

100-Penny Budget Exercise
"How Would You Spend Your City Tax Dollar?"

Created by Lyn Menne & Linda Harris
For Decatur 101
Decatur, Georgia
(Reprinted by Permission)

The City of Decatur, Ga has a relatively higher tax rate than most other municipalities in the Atlanta metropolitan area. Because the City has its own independent school system and tax bills include both school and city taxes, many property owners don't differentiate between the amount allocated to the school system and the amount billed by the City of Decatur. Since 68% of every tax dollar goes to the school system and only 32% goes to the City our goal was to create an interactive exercise in the Decatur 101 curriculum that illustrated the significantly smaller percentage that was billed by the City. We wanted participants to appreciate how many city services were funded by that 32% and how difficult it was to provide a high level of service with limited resources and without raising taxes. We wanted to see if participants would spend their city tax revenue the same way the City actually allocated it. It was important that it be tangible, fun and allow participants to work in small groups to appreciate the challenge of funding competing interests and give them a chance to interact with each other.

Separate the class into small groups of with no more than eight participants. Give each group a bag of 100 pennies to represent 1 tax dollar. Ask group members to count out 68 pennies and set them aside. Once they have done so, tell them they must put those pennies back in the bag because they belong to the school system and cannot be used for city services. They can now see that they only have 32 pennies to spend on all city services. Give each group a flip chart with the list of city departments and ask them to allocate the pennies accordingly. Remind them that personnel costs are figured into the pennies and are not a separate category. (Hint: departments with more people need more pennies). Let each group discuss among themselves how they want to assign their pennies between the various departments. Remind them that if they want more than 32 pennies, they have to raise the millage rate. Rotate among the groups and answer questions as they arise. Once each group as reached agreement on how they would divide the 32 pennies, have each group report out. Then show them a list of how the city actually spends a city tax dollar.

It sounds simple but it is very effective. It is important that they actually count out the pennies and tangibly feel how much goes to the school system. This exercise clearly illustrates that the City actually has control over a very small percentage of the tax bill and citizens should consider attending board of education budget hearings in addition to meetings about the City budget. The general reaction among participants is surprise at how much the city funds with only 32% of the tax bill, how little is allocated to quality of life programs and how much of the budget is controlled by personnel costs. Typically we find that participants under fund larger departments like police and public works which employ the largest number of city employees and they over fund programs like recreation and downtown development. It isn't unusual for groups to decide a tax increase is in order because they basically want more of everything we do.

5. The End Is Just the Beginning: Graduation and Engaging Alumni

The Alameda County Leadership Academy provided beneficial insight into our county's programs, operations, and general management that all residents and voters should be aware of. I have a more educated perspective on issues that impact me as both an Alameda County resident and a public administrator—and feel like a more responsible citizen for participating in this program. I highly recommend it to others.

Alameda County, California, alum

Once a program has run its course and participants have completed the requirements outlined in the curriculum, it is time to celebrate the commitment and effort involved in completing the program. Having a graduation ceremony of some kind is a common way whereby programs show appreciation for the citizens who took time out of their busy schedules to participate in the citizens academy. It can also be a symbolic demonstration of the value that a local government places in fostering an informed and engaged citizenry.

Throughout the program and at graduation, local government staff can plant seeds of encouragement for participants to consider continuing community engagement in other capacities. Long after the last lesson is completed and diplomas are distributed, graduates of the program should feel comfortable conversing knowledgeably about local affairs and empowered to serve on citizen advisory committees and boards or in some other capacity.

This chapter provides an overview of common practices for hosting a commencement ceremony for program graduates, followed by examples of ways that alumni can continue to be engaged and leveraged in terms of building the community's civic infrastructure.

Recognizing Participants' Efforts through Graduation

Most citizens academies (the majority of which follow the cohort model with a set track of sessions) feature some kind of formal graduation ceremony for participants at the end of the program. Often, a nice reception or even dinner is held for the graduates. Some programs include formal recognition of graduates during council or board meetings. Regardless of how it is done, recognizing participants and honoring them for their commitment is an important aspect of the program.

Leadership scholars Jim Kouzes and Barry Posner highlight the importance of showing appreciation for individual effort and contribution as well as publicly celebrating accomplishments in their best-selling book *The Leadership Challenge* (2012). Taking time out to congratulate participants and publicly recognize their effort shows that an organization cares about and honors participants' efforts

Graduation cake served at the Clearwater (Fla.) 101 graduation ceremony (Photo by City of Clearwater)

Graduates of the Raleigh (N.C.) Neighborhood College tossing their mortarboards at city hall. A formal cap and gown ceremony is one way of honoring the effort participants put into the program. It also communicates to participants that the program is a "big deal" to the city and underscores the value of their continued engagement as "alumni."

while also reinforcing the public values of engagement and local democratic participation generally.

One of the final gatherings for the Addison, Texas, Citizens Academy is held during a town council meeting with council members and other town officials in attendance. The Raleigh Neighborhood College holds its graduation reception in the city council chambers and has participants dress in caps and gowns. The Greensboro City Academy also holds its graduation reception in the city council chambers. Conversely, the graduation ceremony for the Alameda County, California, Citizens Academy is held during the final session of the program, which largely focuses on informing participants about the various ways they can get involved in their community moving forward and is directly followed by a celebratory reception.

Other programs elect to hold more formal graduation receptions. In the past, Fort Smith, Arkansas, has held a dinner at a local community center to honor program graduates and extends a separate invitation to the event. Regardless of the location, most programs encourage family members and friends to attend, and many feature an outside graduation speaker as well as the mayor or a county commissioner offering remarks.

Alexandria (Va.) City Academy 2016 graduates receive their certificates from the mayor and city manager in a formal ceremony held in council chambers

In terms of provisions, the section on budgeting in Chapter 2 outlined that food and gifts should be worked into the overall cost of the program from the outset. Most programs provide food at the graduation ceremony, even if they do not normally do so at regular sessions, and many have the event catered. Most programs hand out some type of certificate, whereas more expensive diplomas or plaques are less common. Volusia County, Florida, is one program that eliminated plaques as a way to cut the program budget but retains the academy itself. If the budget allows, staff might also consider giving away other gifts to remind graduates of their time at the academy. Such swag could include golf shirts, mugs, paperweights, class photos, stationery, and so on.

Keeping Alumni Engaged

The program is over. Academy alumni leave the final graduation session feeling positive about their experience. They have invested many hours over many weeks and have a newfound appreciation for and understanding of their local government. The next question becomes, now what? How can these citizens be encouraged to maintain their interest in local government and community affairs and become more engaged in their community?

Over the years, program coordinators have kept their alumni engaged in a variety of ways. Beyond keeping in touch, they are finding ways to plug these people into meaningful avenues of participation. Some of the best strategies we have seen employed by successful citizens academies include (1) inviting alumni to apply to openings on advisory boards, committees, and other formal service roles; (2) building an alumni network; (3) using alumni for focus groups and other forms of quick feedback; (4) creating alumni advisory boards for the citizens academy; and (5) encouraging alumni to participate in "next step" programs.

1. Plugging Alumni into Formal Service Roles

One simple strategy for continuing participants' engagement is to set aside time during the program to share information about specific ways citizens can get involved, depending on their level of interest. The average citizen is not aware of the many opportunities there are to serve their community as members of various advisory boards, commissions, and committees. Citizens academies can be thought of as a way of establishing a pipeline of quality candidates for filling such positions.

For citizens academy alumni, these opportunities can be seen as a way of putting their newfound knowledge and perspective to good use. Furthermore, opportunities for community service unconnected to local government could be shared with these groups of civic-minded and (ideally) enthusiastic participants. A simple handout of agencies, departments, and organizations that are interested in utilizing citizens academy graduates could be an invaluable resource for anyone interested in making a difference. If the local government and/or community organizations utilize a volunteer-match website, this could be an opportune time to show people how to use it.[1] Also, in addition to the possibility of serving on local government boards, commissions, and committees, citizens can also learn about other community service opportunities, such as neighborhood associations or local non-profits.

Another way that staff can promote continued civic engagement is to consider potential overlap between application deadlines or election timelines when deciding on the time of year to conduct the program. As noted in Chapter 2, an election presents a great opportunity for participants to become better informed about the local electoral process and how they might be involved. In addition, a program that aligns with the end of a fiscal year provides the opportunity for participants to learn about the budget process and ways they can meaningfully provide input.

---

1. Some representative examples are Volunteer Match (www.volunteermatch.org), Create the Good (www.createthegood.org), United We Serve (www.serve.gov); and Just Serve (www.justserve.org).

The timing can also make the program somewhat of a runway to specific forms of engagement soon after the program ends.

The Cary (North Carolina) School of Government is an example of a program whose annual timing reflects the goal of having its graduates serve on local boards and commissions. A suburb of Raleigh, the state capital, Cary has more than 135,000 residents. Its School of Government was created out of a desire on the part of the town council to "increase understanding of how and when the public is involved in [t]own processes and decisions and spur even greater community involvement." Toward this goal, between 2004 and 2008, the program was offered every fall because town board and commission applications were then due in December (right after the program's conclusion). When that application process was moved to the late spring of each year, the town manager moved the School of Government to early spring so these processes could remain in sync. The program's coordinator, Lana Hygh, reports that the School of Government has indeed become a pipeline for the town in terms of finding enthusiastic and informed citizens to serve on various advisory boards and commissions.

2. Building and Maintaining an Alumni Network

Another relatively easy strategy for keeping alumni engaged is to maintain communication with them. Many programs compile email and snail-mail lists of graduates through which they occasionally reach out to them as a group. In addition to maintaining email and other mailing lists, social media can be an easy way to build an alumni network. However, although many citizens police academies have active Facebook pages, as of this writing, only a few citizens academies leverage Facebook or other social media to build a strong alumni network.

Citizens academies also develop a growing base of residents with whom local government officials can consult and gauge community opinion. Program administrators may choose to invite alumni back to city hall for ad hoc reunion events that align with a particular development in their community. For instance, if the local government is interested in public opinion on whether or not to build a park in a specific community, holding a reunion event leading up to this decision could be a timely opportunity to meet and hear from this informed group. In addition, depending on the size of each class, combining graduates of two or more classes at these events may allow for an exceptional mix of perspectives and viewpoints. It could also give graduates a chance to interact and network with other informed citizens in their community. Chula Vista, California, holds a reunion night for academy graduates every few years to strengthen the post-graduation relationships between staff, elected officials, and program participants as well as to request feedback regarding recent city developments.

Spotlight on the Chula Vista Citizen's Learning Academy

The City of Chula Vista, California, provides a good example of holding post-graduate events to build on what was learned through its Citizen's Learning Academy. The city held reunion nights for both its 2007 and 2008 graduates. The two events, which were held at city hall in June 2008 and February 2009, enabled graduates to reconnect with one another, elected officials, and local government staff while program content was still relatively fresh in their minds. The events also served as forums for the city to elicit feedback on important issues facing the city.

Before the 2007 event, graduates were invited to share their vision of Chula Vista's future in terms of urban development. Program coordinators sent out an email prior to the first meeting that asked participants what their favorite urban place is, and why, and, based on that feedback, invited noted architects to speak at the event. Throughout, graduates were organized into small and large group discussions to share their thoughts on the subject.

At the 2008 reunion event, graduates were educated on the city's current fiscal situation and their input was sought on a proposed one cent sales tax increase as well as potential topics for future reunion events.

Note: This sidebar is drawn from Institute for Local Government, "Citizen's Learning Academy of the City of Chula Vista," www.ca-ilg.org/post/citizens-learning-academy-city-chula-vista (last accessed Aug. 25, 2016).

Citizens police academies (CPAs) tend to do a good job at maintaining an alumni network. Part of this is because community policing programs offer a very direct way for participants to stay plugged-in. It is also likely, because CPAs have been around longer and are much more widespread than citizens academies, that post-academy engagement has become the norm. This suggests that citizens academies can do a better job of building and maintaining alumni networks, even if only through social events.

3. Using Alumni for Focus Groups and Other Feedback

Some program coordinators report utilizing their alumni network as a sort of ready-made audience from which to create focus groups. The Durham Neighborhood College is an in-demand program that has been around for many years. Deborah Craig-Ray, who has coordinated the program for years, reports that contact information for graduates is added to listservs so that they receive news releases and special announcements from the city. Graduates are encouraged to "stay in touch," and some alumni "have created their own independent groups to stay involved." Craig-Ray also notes that "at times we have used graduates to help with special tasks," such as being involved in focus groups "on key issues and initiatives." Clearwater, Florida, is another example of a city that regularly consults small groups of alumni to act as a sounding board on current issues, such as new taxes or program cuts.

4. Creating Alumni Advisory Board for the Citizens Academy

Another way to build on the knowledge and momentum that participants have built up following graduation is to have them guide and improve subsequent programs for subsequent classes. Creating an advisory board made up of alumni from a variety of sessions will offer recent graduates, as well as those graduates who are more removed from the program, the opportunity to reflect on what they have learned about civic engagement. It also will provide these "advisors" with opportunities to offer their own perspectives on how the concepts learned in class have helped them become more involved in local affairs, especially if they have been away from the program for a while. Program staff can collect this first-hand feedback, weigh it against the overall performance goals for the program, and implement it as appropriate.

While the idea of having alumni advisory boards is not exactly commonplace within the citizens academy community, a few programs are catching on to the benefits of this approach to engagement/evaluation. For instance, Rockingham County, North Carolina, has created the Citizens Academy Steering Committee made up of former graduates from multiple classes throughout the program's history. This committee helps provide direction to program leadership, including the county manager, who has detailed his vision of having graduates help the county "do more with less." Since February 2015, the committee chairman has been a graduate of the county's first session held in fall 2012.

Leadership Harnett in Harnett County, North Carolina, is another example of a program that places an emphasis on feedback from graduates to help shape future sessions. Although it is a different program in that it places more of an emphasis on leadership development, is much more intensive, and is a public-private partnership (or hybrid program, as discussed in Chapter 7), it merits special attention here due to its unique governance structure. A board of directors made up entirely of program graduates runs the program, and each session is overseen by at least one board member who works with a subcommittee to plan that session.

"We want our sessions to represent what makes Harnett County such a special place," said Clerk of Court Marsha Johnson, who went through the program in 2012 and (as of this writing) chairs the Leadership Harnett Board of Directors. "We're always striving to improve the program [and are] never satisfied with status quo." One fairly recent addition to the program implemented by the board of directors is the Legacy Project, a service project through which members of each class give back to the community. The Class of 2015 project involved raising money for the Dolly Parton Imagination Library, which provides books for children from birth until age five.

While the level of involvement by the Leadership Harnett Board of Directors is exceptional, it nonetheless serves as a viable model in terms of utilizing alumni. Rather than treat alumni as a passive group of past participants, the board model allows alumni to feel a sense of ownership and responsibility for the program. It also serves to keep the content fresh and engaging and can lift some of the burden off the shoulders of the program coordinator, especially as it relates to marketing the program.

5. Plugging Alumni into Other, Next-Step Programs

The final strategy we wish to discuss here in terms of keeping participants engaged post-graduation involves directing them toward other civic education–type programs offered by a municipality or county. For many alumni, the local citizen's police academy will be the logical next step (if they have not already been through it). For others, another leadership program that acts as an "advanced" citizens academy will help them dive more deeply into developing the skills necessary to become community leaders. As discussed in the previous section, Leadership Harnett is a good example of this type of program.

2016 graduates of Alexandria (Va.) City Academy

The Citizens Leadership Academy (CLA) in Raleigh is another example of a next step opportunity. Graduates of the Raleigh Neighborhood College who show an interest in further developing themselves as civic leaders are eligible to enroll in the CLA, which consists of twelve sessions grouped around three different themes: leadership development, communication dynamics, and asset-based community development. A CLA graduate offered the following testimonial: "I strongly encourage anyone interested in leadership skills to take this course. These are skills that you can take back to your workplace, community, neighborhood, even use in your personal life. If you are thinking of becoming involved in community service in any way, CLA is a must!"

Another way to set participants' expectations toward attending other programs is to structure the initial citizens academy as the first in a series of like programs offered by local government. Ocean City (Maryland) University achieves this by breaking down the number of hours participants are required to commit in order to receive certificates of completion for its basic civic education course (Ocean City University), its citizens police academy, and community emergency response team programs. It then frames the initial 30 hours needed to complete Ocean City University as receiving a "Bachelor's Degree in Municipal Citizenship." For an additional 33 hours, people can take the police academy course and earn their "Master's," with a "Doctorate" available upon completion of the emergency response program. This is a great model for local governments that have the time and resources to maintain these other programs and that are interested in helping to further develop the skills of the people who have already put a significant amount of effort into learning about their communities.

Remember: This Is about Capacity Building

Back in Chapter 1, we discussed the purpose behind the push in recent years by many local government officials to implement citizens academies and encourage citizens to take a more active role in shaping their communities. This movement toward promoting better informed, more engaged members of society, as well as the underlying reasoning behind it, have been reported on by public administration scholars Jim Svara and Janet Denhardt in an extensive review of the topic commissioned by the International City/County Management Association (ICMA) Alliance for Innovation. According to Svara and Denhardt, civic engagement is seen by many as the "right thing to do" because it reflects the values associated with democratic self-governance and community.[2]

Building civic capacity through citizens academies is the "smart" thing to do also because "effective governance at the local level increasingly requires active and ongoing citizen participation" as "the complexity of the problems facing local government demands citizen involvement and acceptance, if not cooperation."[3] If the ultimate goal is to get citizens to participate more fully in civic affairs, the training provided to them through citizens academies should prepare them for, and encourage in them, this pursuit. Graduation ceremonies and guidance on various ways to get involved as well as continuous relationship building in the post-graduation period are essential ways that local governments can build and

---

2. James H. Svara and Janet V. Denhardt, eds., "Connected Communities: Local Governments as a Partner in Citizen Engagement and Community Building," white paper (Phoenix, Ariz.: ICMA Alliance for Innovation, Oct. 15, 2010), 6–7, http://icma.org/en/icma/knowledge_network/documents/kn/document/301763/connected_communities_local_governments_as_a_partner_in_citizen_engagement_and_community_building.
3. Svara and Denhardt, "Connected Communities," 7.

maintain a steady stream of individuals interested in contributing to the public good.

Never forget that citizens academies are about more than giving local government officials the opportunity to play "show and tell" in front of a group of citizens. Above all, it is about building civic capacity for authentic civic engagement one citizen, or one cohort, at a time. It is therefore vitally important, once that flame is lit, to keep the fire burning.

Questions to Consider

(For new programs) How will you keep track of alumni after the program is over?

_____

_____

What opportunities can you (or do you?) create for alumni to stay engaged after the program is over?

_____

_____

At the end of the program, how can you best steer soon-to-be graduates toward volunteer opportunities or even formal service roles on boards, commissions, committees, and so forth?

_____

_____

How can you honor participants in a way that really shows them how grateful you are for their time and dedication?

_____

_____

How can a graduation or other recognition event show genuine appreciation and help create a spirit of community?

_____

_____

Are there other programs (such as police or fire academies or leadership programs) being offered by local government or other community organizations that could provide a next-step opportunity for program graduates?

_____

_____

Appendix 5   Exhibit Items

Exhibit 5.1   Greensboro City Academy Graduation Invitation

GREENSBORO

Your presence is requested at the
graduation of the

2014 City Academy Class

Tuesday, November 18, 2014

5:30 pm

at the Melvin Municipal Office Building
300 West Washington Street
City Council Chambers

*A reception will be held from 4:30 to 5:30 pm
in the Plaza Level Conference Room.*

*Please join us as we honor the
Graduating class of*

City Academy 2014

6. Is Your Program Working? Aiming for Meaningful Evaluation

> *I have developed a much greater appreciation for our city and the individuals hired to perform various tasks. I now promote to others how great our city really is and why being involved with a program such as City Academy can shed an entirely different light on your views about our wonderful city.*
>
> Participant of the Greensboro (North Carolina) City Academy

While there are numerous similarities across citizens academies, there is also a great deal of variation around the particulars. Some programs are relatively short (6 to 10 hours) while others are much longer (30 to 40 hours). Some offer a meal each time, others do not. Some require a registration fee, while most do not. Regardless of these differences, what we hear from dozens of program coordinators across the country is that they feel positively about their programs; they view them as successful. They report positive feedback from citizens. They note how program alumni become ambassadors for the local government out in the community. They note how many participants end up serving in volunteer capacities in local government or even end up running for office.

In theory, citizens academies help meet broad public-sector goals of enhanced citizen understanding of government, civic engagement, and even enhancing civic trust. And the anecdotal evidence suggests that, by and large, most programs are at least somewhat successful in advancing these goals. But how can a specific program, in a specific place, know whether its goals are actually being accomplished?

In other words, how can success be measured? Finding a meaningful way of evaluating citizens academies is critical to determining whether or not the investment is worth it.

Harvard public policy professor Robert Behn explains that "leaders of public agencies can use performance measures to achieve a number of very different purposes, and they need to carefully and explicitly choose their purposes. Only then can they identify or create specific measures that are appropriate for each individual purpose." Behn makes the case for public sector performance measurement as a way "to evaluate, control, budget, motivate, promote, celebrate, learn, and improve."[1]

David Ammons, a UNC Chapel Hill professor and a leader in the area of measuring public performance, has written extensively on the subject. He notes that proponents of local government performance measurement "have promised that more sophisticated measurement systems will undergird management processes, better inform resource allocation decisions, enhance legislative oversight, and increase accountability."[2] When this practice is applied to citizens academies, it means that program staff have an opportunity to better determine the extent of program "success" but also to demonstrate to the community that the public investment in such a program is worthwhile.

Measuring Performance and Organizational Learning

Performance management, also called results-based management, is an approach to public management that emphasizes the efficiency and effectiveness of public programs as well as the gathering of information on program outputs and outcomes as a means of enhancing decision making that leads to greater organizational effectiveness. When properly applied, this process increases the accountability and credibility of public enterprises. When we consider citizens academies as discretionary local government programs (drawing on limited resources, most prominently staff time), we see how important it is to carefully evaluate outputs and outcomes to determine whether and to what extent program goals are being achieved.

---

1. Robert D. Behn, "Why Measure Performance? Different Purposes Require Different Measures." *Public Administration Review* 63, no. 5 (2003): 586–606; quotes at 588.

2. David N. Ammons, "Overcoming the Inadequacies of Performance Measurement in Local Government: The Case of Libraries and Leisure Services." *Public Administration Review* 55, no. 1 (1995): 37–47; quote at 37.

Figure 6.1   Performance Management Life Cycle

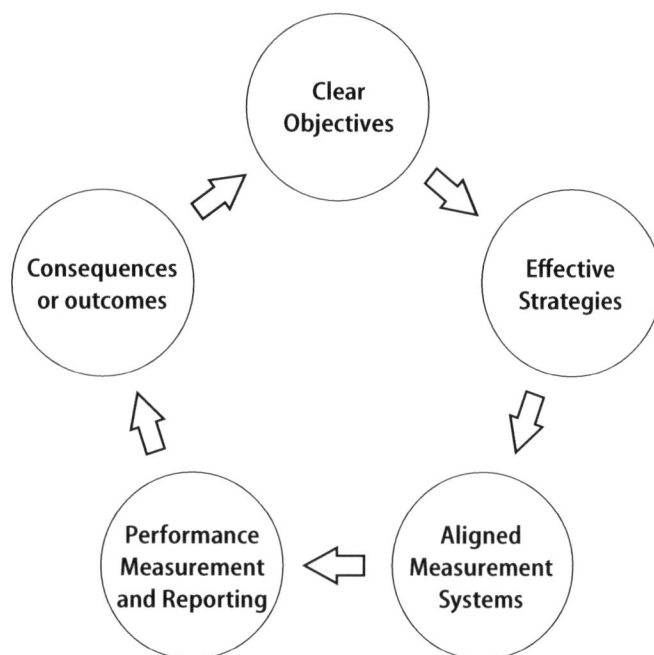

Re-created from James C. McDavid, Irene Huse, and Laura R. L. Hawthorn, *Program Evaluation and Performance Measurement: An Introduction to Practice*, 2nd ed. (Thousand Oaks, Calif.: Sage, 2012).

The evaluation and measurement of citizens academy programs can occur at any phase of the program's life cycle. The authors of *Program Evaluation and Performance Measurement: An Introduction to Practice* (2012) describe public sector performance management as having a five-step life cycle (see Figure 6.1) starting with the development of clear, strategic objectives and cycling through to the application of lessons learned to help future iterations of the program become more successful than the last.[3] As briefly discussed in Chapter 2 of this handbook, linking intended citizens academy outcomes with overall organizational objectives at the outset can help ensure that the program supports the overall goals of the organization. Prior to program implementation, staff should assess these objectives and determine how the goals of the program fit in with the overall vision and mission of the organization. The information gleaned from such an assessment

---

3. James C. McDavid, Irene Huse, and Laura R. L. Hawthorn, *Program Evaluation and Performance Measurement: An Introduction to Practice*, 2nd ed. (Thousand Oaks, Calif.: Sage, 2012).

can help citizens academy staff develop specific, measurable strategies that will align with their chosen objectives.

Peter Senge of the MIT Sloan School of Management has famously written about learning organizations that "continually enhance their capacity to fully realize their highest aspirations."[4] The way citizens academies are run and evaluated can be part of an overall organizational learning system through which programs and services are regularly evaluated in order to inform practice and ultimately improve over time in the name of better serving citizens. Senge talks about the need for systems thinking to help learning organizations establish a conceptual framework for conducting evaluations and using the information after it has been gathered. Rather than have evaluators consider just a single snapshot, this framework encourages them to be mindful that they are bound to "invisible fabrics of interrelated actions" and to contemplate the entire pattern of change that may take place over a span of years.

How does an organizational learning framework apply to citizens academies? At the very least, it suggests that program staff should not only evaluate each iteration of the program, but that they should also take these individual program snapshots and compare them over a span of years to measure patterns of change that otherwise might not have been discoverable. It also suggests that, ideally, staff should evaluate the same group of graduates at pre-established intervals extending well beyond graduation day.

For instance, consider that some graduates may not end up serving on local boards and commissions or take on other community leadership roles until a year or more after finishing the program. A single snapshot (evaluation) administered just after their last program session will not be able to fully measure the impact the program had on enhancing citizen involvement within the community. Perhaps most important, though, is the practice of learning from evaluation and feedback so that improvements (both large and small) can be made such that the program is ever evolving toward greater effectiveness.

The importance of taking the time to carefully evaluate program outputs and outcomes and determine to what extent goals are being achieved (perhaps over a span of a few years) cannot be overstated. Performance management offers up specific information-gathering methods that can be useful for program staff who want these answers, but it is not as simple as administering periodic evaluations to citizens academy participants/graduates and hoping for the best. Citizens academies

---

4. Peter M. Senge, *The Fifth Discipline: The Art and Practice of the Learning Organization*, rev. ed. (New York: Broadway Books, 2006).

Spotlight on Greensboro (North Carolina) City Academy

Greensboro, North Carolina, takes a performance management approach to conducting its City Academy. Academy staff encourage presenters from the participating departments—Human Relations, Parks and Recreation, and Transportation, among others—to make their respective sessions interactive and engaging so that participants are informed about their local government in a stimulating, hands-on environment (see Chapter 4 for more information on the importance of experiential learning). In addition, the city clerk briefs participants about local boards and commissions and provides information on how to apply.

The process of helping City Academy participants understand the work of various departments while also showing them how they can put their newfound knowledge to good use within their communities is directly in line with the program's mission: to develop future leaders and to build a better community by fostering civic engagement, with a particular focus on serving on a local board or commission. The program's mission directly connects to the City of Greensboro's mission statement "to partner with the community to build the desired quality of life for Greensboro." City Academy serves as a testament to the city's dedication to partnering with residents in shaping the community by providing the necessary foundation for an engaged citizenry.

City Academy uses evaluations to assess whether its experiential learning strategies are achieving the academy's intended goals of meeting the City of Greensboro's overall objective of engaging more citizens in public service. Program staff distribute a series of summative evaluations to participants at the end of each session for two purposes: to reward the departments whose presentations were said to be among the best and to help the lowest scorers improve their sessions the next time around. Trophies are awarded to the highest ranking department as well as to the participants' favorite instructor. This is directly related to another overall mission of the city: to maintain "a work environment which fosters employee commitment to public service and making a difference in the lives of our residents."

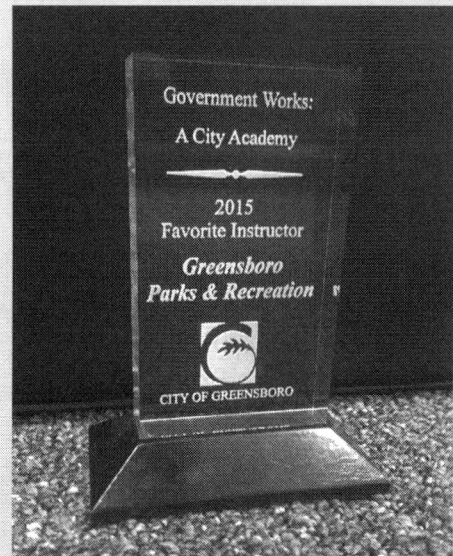

have to be dedicated to leveraging the information they gather to make innovations to the current program structure in the name of providing a better experience for citizens. This is the whole idea behind learning organizations. In order to apply a learning perspective to their program, organizers have to be willing to learn from past failures and to actually apply these key findings in the future. (See sidebar spotlighting the Greensboro City Academy.)

Designing Participant Surveys

However they are constructed and administered, evaluations should focus on determining to what extent the program in question is creating desired outcomes. *Program Evaluation and Performance Measurement* (discussed above) calls for a holistic approach to evaluating a program at all phases of its life cycle. Evaluations tend to include a wide array of questions, and McDavid et al. provide several possible evaluation questions to help organizers start thinking about how to measure their program's performance (see Table 6.1).

In McDavid et al.'s performance management life cycle (see Figure 6.1), we can see that the process both begins and ends with the development of clear, strategic objectives. Planning staff should ask probing questions that (1) assess the *need* for a citizens academy in either the "clear objectives" phase or the "effective strategies" phase, since both seek to discover the degree to which the program, as it stands, is capable of fulfilling the outlined objectives. In addition, questions are needed that (2) focus on the *appropriateness* of the program's structure for addressing these objectives and how well the tactics for accomplishing the stated objectives are working. Additional questions are needed to (3) examine how the program is *implemented* within the community. These are questions that typically would be found in an after-session evaluation. The final two questions listed in Table 6.1 fall into the fourth step of the performance management cycle, the "performance measurement and reporting" phase. These questions reflect a desire to gain information about (4) whether the program *achieved* its intended objectives and, finally, (5) whether the program can be considered *cost-effective* in terms of accomplishing its overall purpose.

By now we have reiterated multiple times that performance evaluations are critical tools for determining whether an organization's community engagement goals are, or can be, accomplished through the citizens academy program (e.g., whether the program is inspiring citizens in ways that will lead them to apply to serve on boards and commissions). However, we have only briefly discussed the population that program staff should be tailoring these evaluations toward.

Table 6.1   Possible Evaluation Questions for All Phases of a Program's Life Cycle

Possible Questions

1. What is the *need* for a citizen's academy in your community?
2. Is the citizens academy structure/logic *appropriate* for addressing these needs?
3. Was the citizens academy *implemented* as intended?
4. Did the citizens academy *achieve* its intended objectives?
5. Was the program *cost-effective*?

Adapted from James C. McDavid, Irene Huse, and Laura R. L. Hawthorn, *Program Evaluation and Performance Measurement: An Introduction to Practice*, 2nd ed. (Thousand Oaks, Calif.: Sage, 2012).

One way that many programs start to assess their effectiveness is by involving program participants in evaluating the quality of individual sessions right after they occur. Hillsborough and Durham in North Carolina are among the many cities that follow this evaluation structure. The Neighborhood College in Raleigh also distributes evaluations immediately following the conclusion of each session (to ensure that lessons are still fresh in participants' minds). Staff then take the time to assess this data and identify any shortcomings that can help strengthen the program moving forward. As shown in the sidebar spotlighting the Greensboro City Academy, this program also follows the model of asking participants to evaluate their experience at the end of each session. A sample end-of-session evaluation is presented in Figure 6.2.

On the other hand, some programs, such as Decatur 101, prefer to wait until the last session of the program to ask participants for their opinions on the program as a whole. Waiting until the end to evaluate could be an opportune moment to gather feedback on whether the overall program has, for example, inspired any of the participants to apply for local advisory boards and commissions post-graduation. In addition, some programs may use the end-of-program evaluation as a tool to encourage interest among soon-to-be graduates in serving on alumni focus groups and inviting their neighbors and friends to apply to later programs. A sample end-of-program evaluation is presented in Figure 6.3.

In addition to the individual "in the moment" evaluation and the overall "after the fact" evaluation, a couple of other options for assessing program performance are worth mentioning. Program staff might consider combining the benefits of multiple post-session evaluations with the benefits of a single overall evaluation. The upside to conducting individual session–only evaluations in addition to an overall program evaluation at the end is that staff will have a better chance of

Figure 6.2   Sample Evaluation Questions: Session-by-Session

1. Please rate the overall quality of today's session:

Poor	Fair	Good	Very Good	Excellent

2. Please rate the overall quality of the presentations led by each presenter:

Presenters' Names	Poor	Fair	Good	Very Good	Excellent

3. How satisfied were you with the following logistical aspects of today's session?

	Satisfied	Neutral	Dissatisfied	N/A
Session Location(s)				
Session Time				
Session Duration				
Group Activities (if any)				
Refreshments				

Please provide any comments you have related to program logistics:

4. To what extent do you feel you learned something new during this session?

Strongly Disagree	Disagree	Neutral	Agree	Strongly Agree

5. What did you like best about this session?

6. What, if anything, could have been done to make this session more worthwhile?

7. How will you use what you have learned in the future?

piecing together a more complete picture of the program's successes and failures. For instance, if, on the final overall evaluation, most people report being only "somewhat knowledgeable" of town/county operations, staff could refer back to the individual session evaluations to try and pinpoint the session (or sessions) that need improvement. One downside to conducting that many evaluations throughout the course of a program is that it might lead to "evaluation fatigue." If program participants grow weary of filling out forms and become less invested in putting

Figure 6.3   Sample Evaluation: End-of-Program

1. How well do you feel the citizens academy program achieved the following program objectives and outcomes?

Objectives	Poor	Fair	Good	Very Good	Excellent
Increased my knowledge of local government					
Improved my ability to participate in and have a positive influence on local government					
Increased my understanding of ways that I can serve my community					
Increased my desire to serve in my community					

Outcomes	Strongly Disagree	Disagree	Neutral	Agree	Strongly Agree
I better appreciate the range of services provided by local government					
I feel more confident in approaching city/county staff with questions or concerns					
I feel more equipped to participate in discussions about community issues					
I felt the classroom conditions were comfortable and appropriate (including any areas where I participated in field trips)					

2. How would you rate your knowledge of town/county operations?

	Not at all knowledgeable	Slightly knowledgeable	Somewhat knowledgeable	Moderately knowledgeable	Extremely knowledgeable
Before the program					
At end of program					

3. What specifically did you like most about the program?

4. What specifically did you like least about the program?

5. Are there other topics you would have liked to have covered?

(*continued*)

Figure 6.3   Sample Evaluation: End-of-Program (*continued*)

Post-Graduation Plans

6. Would you be willing to serve on an advisory board or commission   Yes   No
in the future?

If yes, do you know which you are most interested in?

On a planning group for future town/county projects?   Yes   No

7. Would you tell your neighbors/peers/friends/family to sign up for   Yes   No
the program?

8. Are you planning on staying in touch with at least one person in   Yes   No
your cohort?

9. Do you have a specific interest or skill that you would enjoy using to help the town if it
was ever needed? If so, what would your interest or skill be?

10. What other feedback would you like to share with the citizens academy program
staff?

forth the effort to complete them as the weeks go by, the final overall evaluation may not end up being an accurate reflection of the program's impact on them.

Another evaluation option may be particularly useful for program evaluators who want to avoid creating "evaluation fatigue" but also want to retain some of the benefits of conducting both types of evaluations. This option involves administering a single evaluation at the end of the program but including within it an opportunity for soon-to-be graduates to reflect on their experiences of each session. This evaluation will most likely be longer than a typical overall evaluation form and might look similar to a combination of the two types. As discussed above, one key benefit of the individual session evaluation is that it enables program staff to pinpoint specific areas in need of improvement moving forward. However, the ability of participants to reflect meaningfully on each presentation (that is, to remember the specifics of each session) decreases as time passes. Coordinators who decide to include individual session evaluations within the overall end-of-program evaluation need to include reminders of who taught what class and what interactive exercise was featured in each in order to jog the participants' memories.

Figure 6.4   Four Possible Methods of Evaluating Citizens Academies

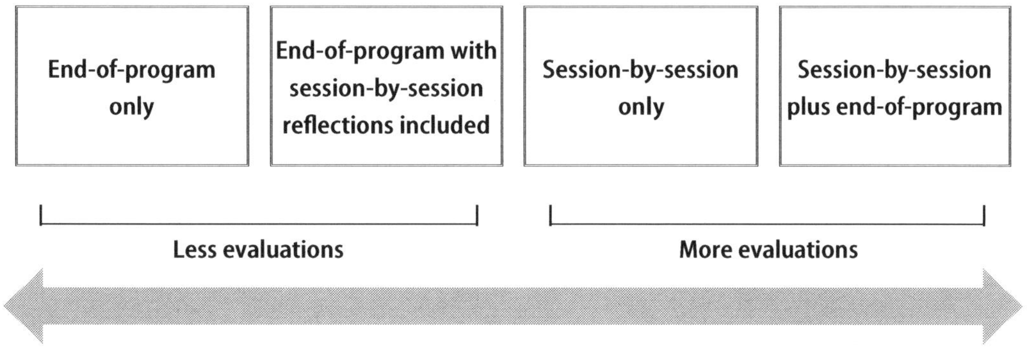

Conclusion

In this chapter we have highlighted four processes for conducting citizens academy evaluations: (1) after each individual session, (2) an overall assessment conducted at the end of the program, (3) session-by-session evaluations in addition to the overall end-of-program assessment, and (4) an overall end-of-program evaluation that includes participants' reflections of each individual session. These four options are illustrated in Figure 6.4, which demonstrates the range of options, from more to fewer evaluations.

Keep in mind that these four methods for evaluation are just a small sampling of the possible options for assessing a citizens academy. Ultimately, the methods a program adopts should depend on the program structure, participant availability, and even the capacity of program staff to properly assess each evaluation after it has been completed. For instance, some programs with alternative formats (such as those that have a single Saturday session) will not benefit from a session-by-session evaluation. On the other hand, end-of-program sample questions that measure overall aspects, such as, "Would you tell your neighbors/peers/friends/family to sign up for the program?" and "What specific things did you like most about the program?" should be helpful to most programs regardless of their format. Sample evaluations implemented by some exemplary citizens academy programs, such as Durham, North Carolina (session by session), Ocean City, Maryland (end of program), Hillsborough, North Carolina (end of program, including individual sessions), Clearwater, Florida (end of program), and Chatham County, North Carolina (end of program, including individual sessions), are presented in Appendix 6.

A successful citizens academy goes beyond adopting appropriate logistical elements, diverse methods to recruit the right participants, and interesting and engaging content. It also establishes a meaningful method of evaluation to gauge whether the program is actually accomplishing program goals as well as satisfying the needs of community members. A citizens academy program can fit within a performance management paradigm and be evaluated like any other public program. Program staff need to think about questions that should be asked at each phase of the program and be prepared to initiate periodic program improvements as a result of these key learnings.

Moving forward, researchers and evaluators searching for more in-depth ways to gauge whether citizens academies are meeting the purported goals of enhancing civic participation are looking to the next generation of program evaluation methods for guidance. *Longitudinal studies* constitute a key component of this next-generation approach. Although this type of evaluation is being mentioned only briefly here, it fits into the conceptual framework that encourages learning organizations to contemplate the entire pattern of change within a program rather than simply consider a single snapshot. Systems thinkers can use longitudinal studies to evaluate a program over a longer span of time than merely right after each session or program. This approach would require citizens academies to "follow" a group of participants for years after graduation in order to get a better sense of the impact that their participation has had on their civic participation.

Another next-generation approach to evaluations is the *quasi-experimental approach*, which could be used to compare the effects of getting a citizens academy education (the "treatment group") with not getting a citizens academy education (the "control group"). A drawback to these research designs is that they require a level of control over the program and its environment that would be difficult to achieve without "modifying existing administrative procedures and perhaps even temporarily changing or suspending policies (e.g., to create no-program comparison groups)."[5] Nevertheless, exploring innovative evaluation methodologies would be a promising way to evaluate outcomes in a way that standard evaluations simply cannot.

Whatever type of evaluation a program chooses to implement, participant feedback is vital for understanding program performance and impact. Providing participants with an opportunity to share their opinions on various aspects of the program, such as curriculum, timing, location, and overall satisfaction, not only makes them feel like their opinions are valued, but it can also be an opportunity

---

5. McDavid, Huse, and Hawthorn, *Program Evaluation and Performance Measurement*, 29.

for staff to collect ideas for improvement that they may never have thought of otherwise. In other words, beyond being able to say whether or not a program's objectives have been met, taking time to gather participants' feedback is an important source of learning and is vital to being able to continually improve the program.

Questions to Consider

How does your organization evaluate other programs or otherwise measure program performance and outcomes?

_____

_____

What are the goals and objectives for your program? How might you best measure the extent to which they are being achieved?

_____

_____

What feedback would be useful for coordinators and staff presenters to have in order to continually learn and improve the program?

_____

_____

Considering the range of methods and timing for evaluating citizens academies, which approach makes the most sense for your program, given the answers to the questions above?

_____

_____

What will you do with the data you collect?

_____

_____

Appendix 6   Exhibit Items

Exhibit 6.1   Ocean City (Maryland) University Evaluation and Course Survey Form (overall course)

OCEAN CITY UNIVERSITY
EVALUATION AND COURSE SURVEY

1. Did the courses properly cover the information as outlined in the course descriptions?
    _____Yes   _____No
    Comments:_____
    _____

2. Were the instructors knowledgeable and informed on their subject?
    _____Yes   _____No
    Comments:_____
    _____

3. Were the handouts for the courses helpful?
    _____Yes   _____No
    Comments:_____
    _____

4. Did you find the classroom conditions comfortable and appropriate? This includes any areas where you participated in "field" trips.
    _____Yes   _____No
    Comments:_____
    _____

5. For the topics covered in the semester you attended, was there anything additional you believe would enhance the course offerings?
    _____Yes   _____No
    Comments:_____
    _____

6. Would you recommend Ocean City University to others?
    _____Yes   _____No
    Comments:_____
    _____

7. Do you have any suggestions that you feel would improve the OCU experience?
    _____Yes   _____No
    Comments:_____
    _____

8. Are there any comments you would like me to share with the Mayor and Council on graduation night?
    _____
    _____
    _____

PLEASE RETURN TO:
Diana Chavis, City Clerk
P.O. Box 158, Ocean City, MD   21843
Or via email dchavis@oceancitymd.gov

Exhibit 6.2   Clearwater (Florida) Citizen's Leadership Academy—Clearwater 101—Evaluation Form (overall course)

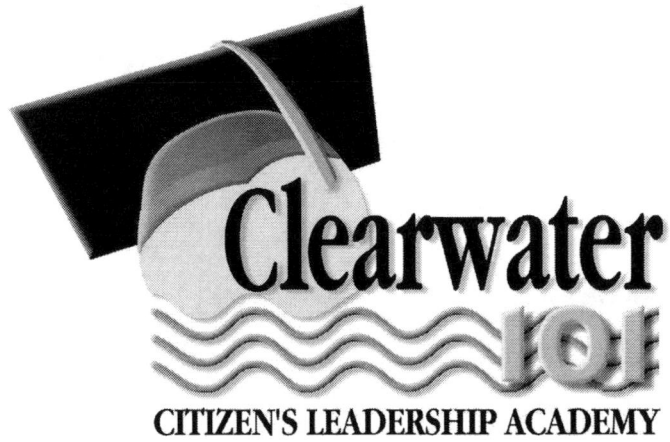

FINAL EXAM

**Exhibit 6.2   Clearwater (Florida) Citizen's Leadership Academy—Clearwater 101—
Evaluation Form (overall course) (*continued*)**

Clearwater 101: Citizens Academy Program

Please take some time to let us know what we could improve upon for next year's class!

1. Which presentation did you enjoy the most?

2. Which did you enjoy the least?

3. Which session was the most informative?

4. Is there anything you think we should drop?

5. Which sessions would you have liked to be longer?

6. Was there anything we did not cover and should have?

7. Was a ten-week session about right? Would you have been willing to do 12 weeks in order to allot more time to different departments?

8. Please comment on length of class time: Was two and a half hours too long, too short or about right? Would you have been willing to have a 9 p.m. regular ending time in order to accommodate presentations that needed more time?

9. Please rate the dinner/caterer.

10. Is there anything else you wish to add?

11. Are you interested in serving on any City advisory boards, volunteering for city events or future involvement? If so, please give your name here. . . .otherwise you may remain anonymous!

    On behalf of the city of Clearwater, thank you so much for your input and being a part of our Clearwater 101. We hope you continue your learning experience about city government and look forward to hearing from you in the future.

Exhibit 6.3   Hillsborough (North Carolina) Citizens Academy Evaluation Form (overall course, individual sessions)

Citizens Academy Evaluation Form

Final Evaluation

1. **Please rate each of the 7 sessions based on overall quality:**

	Poor	Fair	Good	Very Good	Excellent
Foundation of Government					
Advisory Boards					
Planning					
Utilities System Tour					
Police & Fire					
Town Operations					
Budget Management					

2. **How satisfied were you with the following logistical aspects of the program:**

	Satisfied	Neutral	Dissatisfied
Session Locations			
Durham Tech			
Orange County Public Library			
Orange Rural Fire Department			
Session Time			
Most sessions — 7 to 9 p.m.			
Police & Fire — 7 to 9:30 p.m.			
Utilities Tour — 8 a.m. to 1 p.m.			
Session Duration			
Most sessions — 2 hours			
Police & Fire — 2 hours			
Utilities Tour — 5 hours			
Number of Sessions (7 total sessions)			
Course Pack			
Refreshments			

Please provide any comments you have related to program logistics:

_____

_____

_____

3. **How likely would you be to recommend the citizens academy program to a friend:**

_____ **Very Likely**   _____ **Likely**   _____ **Neutral**   _____ **Unlikely**   _____ **Very Unlikely**

1

Exhibit 6.3   Hillsborough (North Carolina) Citizens Academy
Evaluation Form (overall course, individual sessions) (*continued*)

4. How well do you feel the citizens academy program achieved the following program objectives:

	Very Poorly	Poorly	Adequately	Well	Very Well
Increase citizen knowledge, interest, and ability to influence as well as participate in town government					
Reduce barriers to participating in and influencing town government decisions through increased understanding of key processes and operations					
Assist in building a pipeline of citizens interested in serving the community through future service					
Learn from the citizens attending the academy					

5. How would rate your knowledge of town operations:

	Not at all knowledgeable	Slightly knowledgeable	Somewhat knowledgeable	Moderately knowledgeable	Extremely knowledgeable
Before the program					
At end of program					

6. What specific things did you like most about the program?

_____
_____
_____
_____

7. What specific things did you like least about the program?

_____
_____
_____
_____

8. Are there any recommendations that you have to enhance future citizens academy programs?

_____
_____
_____
_____

2

Exhibit 6.4   Durham (North Carolina) Neighborhood College Evaluation Sheet (individual sessions, each with same format, overall course)

DURHAM

1869
CITY OF MEDICINE

DURHAM COUNTY

Durham Neighborhood College

Evaluation Sheet

Session # 808-Environment   Date: October 31, 2014
Location: City of Durham Neighborhood Improvement Services

Instructions: Please check the box that best represents your feelings toward the following statements:

From the session, I:

	Strongly Agree	Agree	Disagree	Strongly Disagree
1. Gained useful knowledge	☐	☐	☐	☐
2. Believe my time was well spent	☐	☐	☐	☐
3. Believe the materials (handouts, videos, etc.) were of high quality	☐	☐	☐	☐
4. Believe the materials were useful	☐	☐	☐	☐

The department representative(s):

	Strongly Agree	Agree	Disagree	Strongly Disagree
5. Presented the goals and objectives of the department	☐	☐	☐	☐
6. Knew the subject/operations of department	☐	☐	☐	☐
7. Presented ideas clearly	☐	☐	☐	☐
8. Actively involved participants	☐	☐	☐	☐
9. Handled questions effectively	☐	☐	☐	☐

	Very Good	Good	Fair	Poor
10. Overall, I would rate the session	☐	☐	☐	☐

11. What did you find most valuable about this session?

12. What improvement would you suggest?

Exhibit 6.4   Durham (North Carolina) Neighborhood College Evaluation Sheet (individual sessions, each with same format, overall course) (*continued*)

DURHAM
1869
CITY OF MEDICINE

DURHAM COUNTY
1881

Durham Neighborhood College

Overall Evaluation Sheet

Session #9: Case Study and Certification Presentation   **Date: November 7, 2014**
Location: City of Durham City Council Chambers

Instructions: Please check the box that best represents your feelings toward the following statements:

From the session, I:

	Strongly Agree	Agree	Disagree	Strongly Disagree
1. Gained useful knowledge	☐	☐	☐	☐
2. Believe my time was well spent	☐	☐	☐	☐
3. Believe the materials (handouts, videos, etc.) were of high quality	☐	☐	☐	☐
4. Believe the materials were useful	☐	☐	☐	☐

The Case Study Presentations

	Strongly Agree	Agree	Disagree	Strongly Disagree
5. Presented the goals and objectives of Group's case study viewpoint	☐	☐	☐	☐
6. Citizens were engaged in topic	☐	☐	☐	☐
7. Presented ideas clearly	☐	☐	☐	☐
8. Established networking for citizens	☐	☐	☐	☐
9. Case Study topic impacted both City and County Government	☐	☐	☐	☐

	Very Good	Good	Fair	Poor
10. Overall, I would rate Durham Neighborhood College	☐	☐	☐	☐

11. What did you find most valuable about Durham Neighborhood College?

12. What improvement would you suggest for Durham Neighborhood College?

13. Would you recommend Durham Neighborhood College to others to attend? If yes, why? If no, why not?

Thank you for sharing your thoughts and participating in the 2011 Durham Neighborhood College.

Exhibit 6.5   Evaluation Form for the 2015 Chatham County (North Carolina) Citizens' College (overall course, individual sessions)

EVALUATION OF 2015 CITIZENS' COLLEGE

Please evaluate the each of the sessions that you this year. CIRCLE ONE answer per row.

CLASS DATES & TOPICS	OVERALL RATING OF CLASS				
9/24/15 Introductions, Role of Local Government and Elections	Very Good	Good	N/A	Fair	Poor
10/1/15 Library and Cooperative Extension	Very Good	Good	N/A	Fair	Poor
10/8/15 Central Carolina Community College & Chatham County Schools	Very Good	Good	N/A	Fair	Poor
10/15/15 Emergency Ops, Fire Departments & Fire Marshal	Very Good	Good	N/A	Fair	Poor
10/22/15 Sheriff, Police and Courts	Very Good	Good	N/A	Fair	Poor
10/29/15 Planning, Solid Waste & Recycling and Water	Very Good	Good	N/A	Fair	Poor
11/5/15 City & County Management	Very Good	Good	N/A	Fair	Poor

If you could add one or two local government functions during Citizens' College that were not included as part of the agenda, what would they be?

1. _____
2. _____

Which sessions would they replace if we had to remove some to make room for new government topics?

_____
_____

Please provide any other feedback you have to help us improve Citizens' College:

OPTIONAL:

Name: _____

Would you be interested in applying for a county or town committee or board in the future?
Yes____ No____ Not sure____

7. Partnership Models for Citizens Academies

People go in on the first day and they may have seen some of their classmates before, but they feel like they're on their own. By the time they finish, they've really come together as a group and they've made connections that will last a lifetime.

Harnett County Clerk of Court Marsha Johnson,
2012 alumnus of Leadership Harnett

The most common way citizens academies are organized and presented is what we might call a wholly in-house operation. The program is planned, administered, and executed solely by a single unit of local government (whether a municipality, township, or county). Usually a staff member in the manager's (sometimes mayor's) office or in a communications/community relations office coordinates, and all sessions are run by various staff members within the organization. It doesn't have to be wholly in-house, though, as there are promising examples of partnership models worth considering.

This chapter provides a brief overview of three variations of partnership models of citizens academies wherein the program is in some way a collaborative production across organizations. These variations are multi-government, government plus other public organization(s), and government partnership with a non-profit. We first highlight some of the benefits of collaboration in general.

Why Collaboration?

When we talk about collaboration in the production of citizens academies we are talking about working across organizational boundaries to co-produce (i.e., co-create) a program that (ideally) is better than what any individual organization could produce by itself. Partnerships across organizations, sometimes in neighboring jurisdictions, or between government organizations and nonprofits are more and more becoming the norm.

There are three primary reasons to consider a collaborative or partnership approach to conducting a citizens academy. First, the realities of community and local governance tend toward a partnership approach. For citizens, their sense of community is often not coterminous with the boundaries of the local government jurisdiction they live in. One's community identity may be regional, for example. Furthermore, overlapping jurisdictions (e.g., municipalities nested within counties) mean there is no simple one-to-one connection between a citizen's sense of community and a single local government organization.

Further, the realities of governance mean that not only are multiple jurisdictions part of a local community's governance network, but so are other public entities (like school districts or special districts) as well as non-profit entities (like neighborhood organizations, merchants associations, and so on). Thus, if community and local governance are interorganizational, there is a certain logic to having a citizens academy be a co-production of at least some of those organizations. In other words, if the goal is building civic capacity for participation in *local governance* that takes place across an interorganizational network, having the program reflect that interorganizational reality, at least to some extent, makes sense.

If the goal is building civic capacity for participation in local governance, which is an interorganizational process, then having the program reflect that interorganizational reality, at least to some extent, makes sense.

A second logic for collaboration is that, when done well, it can yield a whole that is greater than the sum of its parts. Different organizations offer different strengths and different perspectives. When united by a shared vision, multiple organizations can leverage their differences to create something unique and qualitatively better than what each organization could create by itself. Advocates for collaboration often use the term *synergy* to describe this phenomenon, where "1 + 1 = 3," if you will.

The third reason for a collaborative approach to citizens academies is that these partnerships hold the potential to generate community building benefits *beyond the scope of the program itself.* So in addition to a co-produced program simply offering a better or richer experience for participants, it may well be that

the process of co-producing the program can yield benefits beyond those derived by the participants themselves. Such benefits might be thought of as second- and third-order effects. For example, with collaboration, it is said that "success breeds success." Small wins often lead to larger wins. Thus, when multiple organizations successfully work together to produce and conduct a citizens academy, that success may provide a platform for working together on other things. Working together on the positive goal of establishing a citizens academy can build trust and also give rise to other opportunities to work together. Similarly, participants in co-produced programs may find additional opportunities to make connections outside of their normal community networks. *So a potential result of collaborating to produce a citizens academy could be more community collaboration.*

Partnership Models for Citizens Academies

Of all the innovations we have observed in the design and delivery of citizens academies, perhaps the most promising and impactful is the partnership model whereby two or more organizations work together on program planning and delivery. While each partnership program is unique in its own way, we want to highlight three broad categories that seem most relevant: multi-government, government plus other public organization(s), and government partnership with a non-profit.

Multi-Government Programs

Perhaps the most basic form of partnership is the government-to-government program. Two (or potentially more) neighboring or overlapping jurisdictions team up to offer one program rather than compete for the same audience. The most common and most commonsensical arrangement is the joint municipal-county program. The average citizen likely does not even know which organization does what. Citizens just know that they pay taxes to both entities and utilize services provided by both: from public safety to parks and recreation to libraries and social services. Thus, a combination municipal and county citizens academy is more reflective of the citizens' reality and ultimately can be more useful to them.

Since 2003, the City of Durham and Durham County, North Carolina, have partnered to offer the Durham Neighborhood College. Durham's situation is somewhat unique in that the City of Durham takes up most of the county, with about 82 percent of county residents residing in the city. Over the years, therefore, the two governments have worked together on a variety of services, including the creation and production of the Neighborhood College.

The partnership between the county and city permeates nearly every aspect of the program. Assistant County Manager Deborah Craig-Ray has managed the program for years but works closely with her counterparts at the city to ensure its success. The Neighborhood College commences annually in the fall with a cohort of 30 residents and emphasizes interaction between participants and city and county staff. Participants must be Durham residents and owe no outstanding taxes. Once approved, applicants are selected to make up a class that represents various aspects of Durham's diverse population.

The city and county reserve $6,000 for the program's budget, which is split evenly between the two governments. Each applicant must pay a registration fee of $30 to support the program, but some scholarships are available. A further demonstration of the program's collaborative nature is that sessions sites are equally divided between city and county.

Another example of a municipal-county program is the Montgomery County–Christiansburg Citizens Academy in Virginia. In this case, the Town of Christiansburg, though it takes up only a modest portion of Montgomery County, is the county seat. The emphasis placed on collaboration between the town and county governments is reflected in the following testimonial from a program graduate:

> What I took away from this Academy experience was an increased respect and appreciation for the open and close inter-working of all those involved with Town and County Government positions that share in services, ideas, facilities, equipment and manpower for the benefit of the public. I now have a better understanding of just how much planning, work and dedication actually go into trying to make everything "just right," safe and enjoyable for everyone in the community.

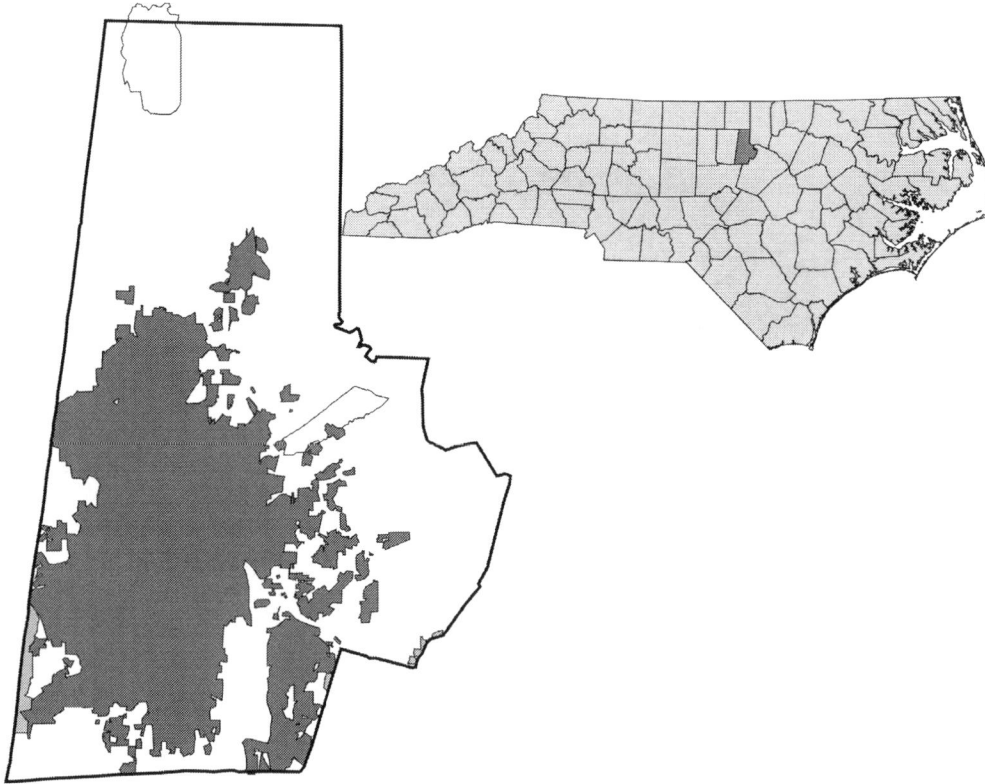

The City of Durham is somewhat unique in that it takes up most of Durham County, as shown here: 85% of county residents live within the city limits of Durham. Since 2003 the city and county have partnered to offer the Durham Neighborhood College.

Begun in 2011, the Montgomery County–Christiansburg Citizens Academy grew out of conversations between the town and county public information officers, both of whom wanted to reach out more and better engage and inform citizens about local government. Each believed that the kind of civic education that was needed was related to local government generally and not necessarily to a specific governmental unit. Together they put together a joint program designed to teach municipal and county government simultaneously.

The first joint program attracted 15 participants. Subsequent cohorts of 20 have taken the program, which meets in the fall in two-and-a-half-hour sessions over eight consecutive weeks. The program is truly a joint production in that some presenters provide information that is relevant to both jurisdictions. For example, one finance department official presents information on the budget process that is applicable to both. In other cases, a session will feature joint representation from

Montgomery County–Christiansburg Citizens Academy participants had their names displayed as bus stops during their visit to Blacksburg Transit (Photo courtesy of Montgomery County, Va.)

the two organizations. For instance, both the sheriff's office and the town police department participate in the session on public safety. The sheriff's office leads a tour of the courthouse, while the police department demonstrates their K-9 corps. Ruth Richey, the county's public information director, notes that "one key to our success is the commitment by both localities to support the program and share the cost and workload. This shared responsibility . . . makes it more affordable and less of a burden on departments, which may have limited staff and time to participate."

Government Plus Other Public Organization(s)

Another type of citizens academy partnership is multi-agency collaboration wherein a local government works with another public entity, such as the cooperative extension service or a community college. Perhaps the most logical multi-agency partnerships are between citizens academies and community colleges, the Chatham County (North Carolina) Citizens' College providing a particularly illustrative example.

In 2005, Chatham County Board of Commissioners helped establish the Citizens' College in partnership with an educational arm of the group Chatham Citizens for Effective Communities (CCEC), which had been promoting the idea. CCEC is self-described as "a citizens action group with the mission of engaging, educating and empowering citizens to enhance Chatham's future." One of the group's board members, Rita Spina, championed the idea of a citizens academy and worked with county staff to design classes and a curriculum that maximized staff participation and was relevant to citizens' interests. Renee Paschal (since that time promoted to county manager) served as the primary county partner.

CCEC formed the CCEC Institute to create and host the new program, to be called Citizens' College. The county provided most of the presenters and booked locations, while Spina handled other logistics and registration. The results were mixed. Some years there were not enough registrants and the program was canceled. One of the challenges was that apparently there was the perception that the program was not unbiased. CCEC was associated with a certain political perspective, and most of the participants of the Citizens' College were either active in CCEC or shared its views. In other words, the program did not have nearly as broad a reach as desired.

Health issues forced Spina to step down as coordinator of Citizens' College in 2011 without a clear successor available from CCEC. Thus, the CCEC Board of Directors and Chatham County saw a natural window of opportunity to re-think the organization of the program. This led to the exploration of a partnership between the community college and the county as primary sponsors and hosts. Several stakeholders noted that having the program offered jointly by Central Carolina Community College (CCCC) and the county government would help allay fears of potential political bias of the curriculum. Further, some felt that if the program were organized and conducted solely in-house that future CCEC board members might not want to continue it. With its large satellite campus in the county seat of Pittsboro, CCCC seemed like a natural partner to help sustain the program and provide it increased legitimacy.

We challenge you to take the knowledge you've gained through this experience and put it to use, whether that is running for elected office, applying to serve on a board or commission in the future, or simply talking to your friends or neighbors about some of the things you've learned. As you choose to move forward, we hope your participation in the Citizens Academy has created a deeper connection with your community and the governments that serve it.

Chair of the Montgomery County (Virginia) Board of Supervisors summing up the goals of the Montgomery County–Christiansburg Citizens Academy, graduation 2012

County staff and a few CCEC board members met with CCCC officials, who were very receptive to the Citizens' College becoming part of its continuing education program. Carl Thompson, a former Chatham County commissioner, led the continuing education program at that time. Thus began the transition of Citizens' College. The first class under the new arrangement was offered in January of 2012 and reached full registration more quickly than in previous years.

The partnership involves the county providing all the planning, coordination, and staffing. The community college registers participants and promotes the program through its continuing education program (see Exhibit 7.1 in Appendix 7). The registration fee is a nominal $25, which covers CCCC's costs (the same fee was charged when it was offered through the CCEC Institute). The program consists of seven, two-and-a-half-hour sessions held in different public facilities. The sessions are very interactive, and topics vary from year to year based on what the "hot" issues are.

Debra Henzey, Chatham County director of communications and point-person for the Citizens' College, outlines several benefits and a few drawbacks of this partnership model.

Benefits

- The program has seen substantial increases in enrollment, with full or nearly full classes every year.
- Both CCCC and the county promote the program, thereby reaching different audiences.
- Those who complete the course can earn class credits.
- CCCC's involvement has resulted in a greater sense of legitimacy and political credibility.
- Related to the above, the program has attracted a greater diversity of students in terms of political views and representation from various areas of the county.
- CCCC has been very good about allowing the class to be held at different locations and being flexible about changes in speakers and topics.

Drawbacks

- It is difficult to change program dates, as a lot of lead time is needed to do so (i.e., less flexibility).
- Some of the paperwork that needs to be handled every year would not be an issue if the program were organized solely in-house.[1]

---

1. Debra Henzey, email communication with author, January 26 and June 28, 2016.

Overall, the benefits seem to be significantly outweighing the drawbacks. The Chatham County Citizens' College is an excellent example of a well-run citizens academy that successfully leverages the different strengths of the county and the community college.

Chatham County is certainly not the only case of a county partnering with a community college to offer a citizens academy. Rockingham County (North Carolina) similarly offers its Citizens' Academy through a partnership with Rockingham Community College (RCC). The setup is different, and not as extensive, but from the outset at least one session has been held on the RCC campus. Furthermore, the application process explicitly states that "all Rockingham Community College students may participate, in or out of County."

Another example of partnering with other public organizations is Monroe County, Indiana. In 2006, the county commissioners launched the Commissioners' Citizens' Academy. Running over eight, two-hour sessions from January through June, the board of commissioners–initiated program was a success from the start. Thirty participants were selected on a first-come, first-served basis in the first year, though at that time the commissioners did most of the recruiting. Some alumni from the first class later went on to serve on various boards and commissions, and a few even ran for local office.

After the initial success, however, the commissioners felt the program was too taxing on the staff's time, so the program went on hiatus for four years. In 2010, some of the local Purdue Extension educators approached the commissioners about taking over the program, since they saw it falling within their education mission. When Purdue Extension began coordinating the program, it continued in its original format and won a local program of excellence award to receive sustained funding. The partnership has continued, and the Monroe County Citizens' Academy is another strong example of a well-run program that leverages the strengths of local government and a public partner. (see Exhibit 7.4 in Appendix 7.)

Government—Non-profit Partnership, or, "Hybrid" Programs

The early version of Chatham County's Citizens' College was a form of government–non-profit collaboration. The program was conducted primarily under the auspices of the CCEC, with the county providing content, until the political associations of the CCEC led the county to take over the program in partnership with CCCC. But in its original form, the citizens college was something of a hybrid program. It was similar to a community leadership program (CLP) (discussed in Chapter 1) in that it focused more broadly on building civic leadership (both inside and outside of government), but it was also like a citizens academy in that most of the content was about local government and was presented by local government officials.

As discussed in Chapter 1, CLPs usually run parallel to citizens academies. CLPs are quite common and are offered by non-profit groups like CCEC, though more often by the chamber of commerce, but also by other civic organizations, such as the League of Women Voters. In most cases, citizens academies run independently of such programs and differ in significant ways (again, highlighted in Chapter 1).

Leadership Los Gatos

Some citizens academy programs are harnessing the power of partnership to deliver joint or even what we might call hybrid programs that offer significant value to both participants and the effort toward civic capacity building. In Los Gatos, California, the local chamber of commerce offers Leadership Los Gatos, which, like most CLPs, is very intensive, meeting across 10, 5-hour sessions. The program costs $400 to attend. So on the surface, Leadership Los Gatos looks more like a CLP than a citizens academy.

But Leadership Los Gatos is different. It is a hybrid program run through a partnership with the Town of Los Gatos for the purpose of promoting "participation and a greater understanding of the workings of our Town and its part in the larger community."[2] Program sessions are very much like those of a typical citizens academy. They cover land use, economic development, education, health, public safety, emergency preparedness, and so on. There are leadership-related sessions on decision-making and communication skills, but the bulk of the programming is clearly geared toward local government. Participants also go on a police ride-along and attend a town council meeting.

What makes the Los Gatos program remarkable is that *it is a community leadership program and a citizens academy combined*. There are no two different programs running in parallel, as is usually the case. It is a true partnership between local government and the chamber of commerce and contains elements of both a typical citizens academy and a typical community leadership program. But unlike a typical citizens academy, topics are covered in greater depth (five-hour sessions as opposed to the more common two- to three-hour sessions). Another difference, as noted above, is that there is a $400 tuition fee for Leadership Los Gatos, whereas most citizens academies are free.

---

2. See the Leadership Los Gatos page of the Los Gatos Chamber of Commerce website, www.losgatoschamber.com/leadership-los-gatos.php.

Leadership Harnett

Harnett County, North Carolina, conducts what may be the longest running hybrid program in the country. It has been around since 1997. Leadership Harnett takes the partnership model to another level, as it has become its own non-profit organization. Unlike other partnerships discussed herein, which have a lead agency running the program in partnership with other groups, the program in Harnett County has evolved into its own partnership organization, complete with a board of directors made up of program alumni that is also representative of the different parties to the partnership.

Leadership Harnett was the brainchild of former County Manager Neil Emory, who had knowledge of a CLP that was run in another county where he had worked, and he believed that Harnett County could benefit from doing something similar. But rather than it being a pure CLP run by the local chamber, Leadership Harnett was conceived as a public–private partnership from the beginning, with the principal partners being Harnett County, area chambers of commerce, and Campbell University.

The programing for Leadership Harnett is much more intensive than that of a typical citizens academy. Applicants must commit to attending all eight sessions (one a month), which run from 7:30 a.m. to 5:00 p.m. Each session involves getting on a bus and touring various key places within the community. Many of the sessions are government related, such as a whole day dedicated to local government and the judicial system, another to health and human services, another to education; a session titled "quality of life" includes a tour of county and state parks and facilities. The program also includes team building activities and, very significantly, a service component. Each class identifies (on their own) a "legacy" service project that involves significant "giving back" to the community.

Anyone can apply to Leadership Harnett, but the process is rigorous. In 2016, there were 34 applicants for 22 slots (the class is always capped at 22). In addition to committing to all eight sessions, applicants are assessed on community interest and involvement, recommendations, demonstrated leadership acumen, and "a willingness to assume expanded community responsibility."[3] (A detailed application is presented in Appendix 7.) The subtitle on the Leadership Harnett

---

3. This quote, and much of this program overview, is drawn from a February 2016 press release titled "Turning Citizens into Leaders: The Legacy of Leadership Harnett," written by Harnett County Public Information Officer Brian Haney, which can be found at www.harnett.org/publicinfo/downloads/2016.02%20Employee%20 Newsletter.pdf.

Members of the 2013 class of Leadership Harnett engaging in a local service project. Its service component is an important element of Leadership Harnett. By working to improve their community, program participants actively build strong relationships with one another.

website is clear enough. It describes the program as a "countywide partnership to develop our county's leadership."[4]

Perhaps the most distinguishing feature of Leadership Harnett's hybrid program is its management and governance. As noted above, a board of directors, made up entirely of alumni, oversees every aspect of the program. The board manages the budget, plans the curriculum, selects participants, and evaluates the program afterward. Members of the board take great pride in improving the program year after year and are at the heart of a strong network of alumni. Members of the board oversee each session and work very hard to pack the almost 10-hour days with interesting and enriching content. See Exhibit 7.2, the "Local Government and Judicial Session Agenda from Leadership Harnett 2015" in Appendix 7.

---

4. See www.leadershipharnett.com.

Although Leadership Harnett is a separate non-profit, the partnership role played by county government is key. At this writing, the 2016 board chair is Harnett County Clerk of Court Marsha Johnson, and the program coordinator is Assistant Register of Deeds Matt Willis.

The benefits of the hybrid model are many. Perhaps the most important are the strong interpersonal connections it builds across the community. As a collaborative endeavor, Leadership Harnett is building an ever-growing network of civic-minded people from all over the county and including all sectors. These individuals plug into government service but also serve, and make connections within the civic arena outside of, local government. In fact, when asked to name the most important contribution made by Leadership Harnett, the most common answer given by board members is the networking—another name for bridging social capital as discussed in earlier chapters of this handbook. People from different sectors and different parts of the county come together and build relationships that they would not have made otherwise. According to Johnson, "People go in on the first day and they may have seen some of their classmates before, but they feel like they're on their own. By the time they finish, they've really come together as a group and they've made connections that will last a lifetime."[5]

Benefits and Drawbacks of the Hybrid Model

There are many clear benefits of the hybrid model as demonstrated by Leadership Harnett and Leadership Los Gatos. First, combining aspects of traditional community leadership programs with citizens academies draws on the strengths of each model, or alternatively, addresses deficiencies with each model. Community leadership programs often do not dive deeply into the intricacies of local government and governance. Yet it stands to reason that effective community leaders are able to successfully understand, navigate, and work effectively with local governments. By the same token, simply knowing about local government may not be enough to enable or empower participants to step into community leadership roles in terms of serving on public boards and commissions, taking an active role in a neighborhood organization, and so on. Augmenting civic knowledge while providing some basics of community leadership would seem to be a super-charged curriculum for a citizens academy.

In addition, hybrid programs can leverage the strengths of the participating organizations to offer a program that more fully meets the needs of the participants. A citizens academy produced solely in-house may become blind to other

---

5. See Haney, "Turning Citizens into Leaders."

A Different Kind of Hybrid Program

League of Women Voters of Charlotte–Mecklenburg Civics 101

Not all non-profit–government partnerships are combinations of leadership programs and citizens academies, as is the case of both Leadership Harnett and Leadership Los Gatos. In the Charlotte, North Carolina, area, the League of Women's Voters (LWV) offers Civics 101, a course focused on local government. Civics 101 was created in 1995 out of a desire to help League members "learn more about how local government really works." Participants meet for five, two-and-a-half-hour sessions: three sessions are held at the Charlotte-Mecklenburg Government Center, where participants hear from representatives of the school system as well as county and city government; one session meets at the courthouse, where the court system is discussed; and the final session is held at the *Charlotte Observer*, where attendees learn about the role of local media and local government. The program is run completely by LWV, but what makes it an interesting hybrid is that most sessions are held at local government venues with local government officials making presentations. Thus, local government is a critical partner in the program even though the program itself is a function of a non-profit organization.

aspects of community governance that are very relevant and important to would-be community leaders. For example, the various functions of government obviously constitute key aspects of community operations, but so does the local business community, including major employers. Thus, a program like Leadership Harnett offers a holistic or broader view of how the community works, thereby introducing participants to a broad array of organizations and dimensions of community beyond local government.

Another strength of the hybrid approach is that programs that adopt aspects of CLPs tend to be more in-depth, with sessions lasting a half or whole day as opposed to a couple of hours. This intensive experience significantly ramps up the social capital building potential of these programs. Participants of Leadership Harnett develop very strong bonds that persist beyond the end of the program. People from all parts of the county who otherwise would probably never have interacted, become friends, thereby building bonds that increase the social capital that is so valuable to civic capacity building. While these results are hard to quantify, they are nevertheless extremely important—likely even more important than the actual knowledge gained in the program.

The main drawback of the hybrid model, at least as presented here, is the difficulty it presents in terms of access and diversity. These programs have an application process that requires the demonstration of serious commitment. Would-be participants must be willing to pay a substantial ($400) fee or have an employer willing to pay the fee or be willing to apply for a scholarship. They must also commit to taking significant chunks of time off during workdays. Such commitments may put these programs out of reach of lower income residents. Scholarships are no doubt helpful, but the reality is that the application process, time commitment, and associated fee are naturally going to be present barriers for a lot of people. Thus, hybrid programs that want to be more widely accessible and broadly representative of the community need to make special efforts to reduce barriers, likely going beyond offering need-based scholarships.

Partnerships—The Future of Citizens Academies?

This chapter has only scratched the surface of potential partnership models for citizens academies. The possibilities are almost endless in terms of the different ways that these programs can be co-produced through partnerships. Multi-jurisdiction partnerships, local government teaming up with another public entity, and local government partnering with non-profits were featured here as they exemplify the more common variations we are seeing. But there are other variations, and it is likely that as citizens academies become more and more commonplace that other types of partnerships will emerge.

While a program created and operated solely in-house is more often than not going to be easier in terms of planning, coordinating, and so on, much can be gained through collaboration. Co-producing citizens academies across organizations potentially offers more perspectives, reaches a broader base of participants, and can be a stronger catalyst for building community networks. Collaboration is not a panacea, however. It is more complicated and can be difficult to pull off, and we would not recommend collaboration for collaboration's sake. Rather, the recommendation here is for coordinators to first consider program goals and, then, whether partnering with other governments and/or community organizations might not help achieve them.

Questions to Consider

What organizations in your community/region might share at least some of the goals your organization has set in terms of civic education?

_____

_____

What local organizations are already doing civic capacity building?

_____

_____

What would your program stand to gain by partnering with another or other organizations to organize and conduct a citizens academy?

_____

_____

What organizations within local government, the public sector, or non-profit community could potentially partner with you in producing a citizens academy?

_____

_____

What are the potential drawbacks of partnering?

_____

_____

What obstacles stand in the way of collaborating with potential partners?

_____

_____

What needs to be done in order to remove or lessen the impact of these obstacles?

_____

_____

Appendix 7   Exhibit Items

Exhibit 7.1   Flier for the Chatham County (North Carolina) Citizens' College

CENTRAL
CAROLINA
COMMUNITY
COLLEGE

CHATHAM COUNTY
NORTH CAROLINA

What the heck is county government?
How does it differ from our towns?
Where do our schools fit into all this?
Get answers, earn CEUs and be more informed!

2013 Chatham County Citizens' College

HOW GOVERNMENT WORKS

Thursday evenings, 6:30-9:00 pm
March 7-April 18, 2013

Chatham County is your home. You may live, work or go to school here. But how much do you really know about how things work in local government?

The Continuing Education class offered through Central Carolina Community College in Pittsboro will help participants:

- Better understand how major county and town services operate and who directs them.
- Explore various options to serve local government as volunteers.
- Get to know key managers and department heads.
- Meet other interested residents in a lively educational format.

The class meets at various locations across the county, including a water treatment plant on Jordan Lake, North Chatham Fire Station and the new Justice Center in Pittsboro.

SIGN ME UP!

CONTINUING EDUCATION CREDITS: 1.75 CEUs earned upon completion

COURSE FEE: $25.00

SCHOLARSHIPS: If you are interested in help paying the registration fee, CCEC - Institute, Inc. generously offers scholarships. Call Debra Henzey at 919-542-8258 for information.

CLASS SCHEDULE: See reverse side.

REGISTER BY FEB. 22, 2013: Call CCCC-Pittsboro Continuing Education to register by phone or to request a hard copy form. Call 919-545-8044.

STILL WANT TO KNOW MORE? Contact Debra Henzey, 919-542-8258 or debra.henzey@chathamnc.org

LIMITED SEATS Sign up early!

Exhibit 7.2   Local Government and Judicial Session Agenda from Leadership Harnett 2015

LEADERSHIP
HARNETT

Local Government & Judicial Session

Wednesday, June 24. 2015

AGENDA:

7:30 a.m.   **Harnett County Jetport – Buies Creek**

Breakfast

Flights, Tour & Presentation   Depart at 9:40 am

10:00 a.m.   **Harnett County Emergency Management**

Gary Pope, Emergency Services Director

Jimmy Riddle – Fire Marshall

Larry Smith – Emergency Management Coordinator

Ricky Denning – EMS Division Chief   Depart at 11:30

11:45 a.m.   **Lunch & Municipal Representatives Forum – Sheriff's Dept - Lillington**

Chairman Harnett County Board of Commissioner – Jim Burgin

Harnett County Manager & Asst. Manager – Joseph Jeffries & Paula Stewart

Angier Mayor – R.H. Ellington

Angier Town Manager – Coley B. Price

Lillington Town Manager – Bill Summers

1:00 p.m.   **Sheriff's Office & Detention Center**

Major Jeff Huber - Presentation & Tour

Lt. Curtis Thompson – Jail Tour - Depart at 2:10

2:20 p.m.   **Harnett County Courthouse**

N.C. Representative Brad Salmon

Harnett County Clerk of Court – Marsha Johnson

Harnett County Register of Deeds   Kim Hargrove

District Attorney – Vernon Stewart

District Court Judge – Resson Faircloth

Veteran's Court Administrator – Ret. Lt. Colonel Mark Teachey

Tax Administrator – Keith Faulkner

5:15 p.m.   **Arrive at Harnett County Jetport**

Breakfast provided by Warren Aviation. Lunch Provided by Sheriff Larry Rollins
Snacks & Drinks provided by the Town of Angier
Committee for Session – Marsha Johnson, Chair – Kim Hargrove – Jenny Harrop – Coley Price – Matt Willis

Exhibit 7.3   Application Form for Harnett County (North Carolina) Leadership 2016

LEADERSHIP
HARNETT

http://www.leadershipharnett.com/

A cooperative effort of Campbell University, and the Angier, Coats, Dunn, Erwin and Lillington Chambers of Commerce.

CONFIDENTIAL APPLICATION

INSTRUCTIONS

Type or print in black ink. Please complete each section fully. Limit answers to the space provided. Application must be signed by both applicant and employer (where applicable) and returned no later than **Friday, January 29, 2016.**

SELECTION CRITERIA

Participation in Leadership Harnett is open to persons living in the Harnett County area.

Participants in Leadership Harnett will be selected by the Selection Committee based upon the information provided in this application. The Committee will seek representation from a cross section of the community to include persons active in the areas of business, education, the arts, religion, government, community-based organizations, ethnic and minority groups.

ATTENDANCE POLICY

Applicants must have the full support of the organization or business they represent. Attendance at Kickoff and Service Project/Wrap-Up sessions are <u>mandatory</u>. Only one session (April-September) absence due to extenuating circumstances (i.e. sickness, death in family) may be excused. **Business conflicts are not considered extenuating circumstances.** No refund of tuition will be made for participants who drop out of the program. No one will graduate from Leadership Harnett without fulfilling attendance requirements.

SUBMITTAL OF APPLICATION

A completed application should be sent to:

> Leadership Harnett Selection Committee
> P.O. Box 507
> Lillington, NC 27546

or

> mwillis@harnett.org

Deadline for receipt of applications is Friday, January 29, 2016

REVISED 12/2015

Exhibit 7.3   Application Form for Harnett County (North Carolina) Leadership 2016 (*continued*)

2016 Leadership Harnett Confidential Application

*Have you ever applied to Leadership Harnett in the past   Yes/No   If so, when? _____

I. PERSONAL DATA

Full Name _____   Name for Name Tag:_____

Home Address

_____
          Street or PO Box   City, State   Zip

Home Telephone ___(_____)_____   Cell Phone ____(_____)_____

Email (where you would like correspondence for the program sent): _____

Length of Residence in the Harnett County Area _____

Gender* _____ Race* _____ Date & Place of Birth* _____
(*Optional information that is helpful in assuring a diverse class.)

Have you ever participated in another state or community leadership program? _____
If yes, name of program(s) & location: _____ When: _____
Do you have any physical disabilities, food allergies or dietary restrictions of which you believe we should be aware? If so, please describe.

_____
_____

II. EDUCATION

	Name/Location of School	Years To-From	Degree	Major
High School				
College				
Graduate				

III. EMPLOYMENT

Current Employer _____ Since _____

Supervisor approving your participation in Leadership Harnett:

_____

Business Mailing Address _____
                Street or PO Box   City, State   Zip

Business Telephone _(_____)_____   Fax ____(_____)_____

Type of Organization/Business _____

Briefly describe your title and responsibilities in your employment:

_____
_____
_____

What do you consider your most significant career achievement to date?

_____
_____
_____

REVISED 12/2015

Exhibit 7.3   Application Form for Harnett County (North Carolina) Leadership 2016 (*continued*)

Business and Professional Affiliations (other than civic organizations and political activities):

Name of Group	Position/Assignments	From	To

IV. COMMUNITY INVOLVEMENT

List community, civic, religious, political, government, social, athletic, or other activities. Do not include business and professional activities.

Organization _____ Dates: _____

Position/Assignment _____

Organization _____ Dates: _____

Position/Assignment _____
(Others may be listed as an addendum to this application, if you wish.)

What do you consider your most important accomplishment to date in the Harnett County community?

_____

_____

_____

V. GENERAL INFORMATION – (This information will be used to plan the 2016 Community Sessions)

Describe what you believe to be the three most significant challenges facing Harnett County.

_____

_____

_____

_____

Describe what you believe to be the three most notable opportunities for the Harnett County area.

_____

_____

_____

What expectations do you have for your Leadership Harnett experience?

_____

_____

_____

_____

REVISED 12/2015

(continued)

Exhibit 7.3 Application Form for Harnett County (North Carolina) Leadership 2016 (*continued*)

VI. Commitment

To graduate from Leadership Harnett, you must attend the Kickoff and Wrap-Up/Service Project Sessions and have missed only one day (combined time) during the community sessions. You are only allowed one excused absence.

I understand the purpose of the Leadership Harnett program and will devote the time and resources necessary to complete the program. I understand the attendance policy as shown on the cover sheet of this application and, in signing this application, agree to be bound by such.

Participants must commit to the following dates:

***Kickoff Session	March 23, 2016	Government/Judicial Session	July 27, 2016
Education Session	April 27, 2016	Quality of Life Session	August 24, 2016
Business/Industry Session	May 25, 2016	Agricultural Session	September 28, 2016
Health/Human Services Session	June 22, 2016	***Service Project/Wrap-up	October 19, 2016

*** - Mandatory Attendance is required for these sessions in order to graduate

Graduation is scheduled for Monday, October 24th, 2016

T-shirt Size _____ (Men's shirt)

Applicant Signature _____ Date _____

EMPLOYER COMMITMENT (if applicable)

This application has the approval of this organization and the applicant has our full support, which includes the time required to participate in the program.

Organization or Firm _____

Signature _____ Title _____

TUITION

The cost of participation in LEADERSHIP HARNETT is $400, which covers all program costs including meals, materials and graduation exercises. Upon acceptance into the program, either you or your employer will be billed for the tuition which must be paid prior to the beginning of the program.

- **Please do not send in tuition with the application. If selected, Leadership Harnett will send an invoice for payment.**

SCHOLARSHIPS

Leadership Harnett understands that some candidates may not be able to take advantage of this leadership experience without tuition assistance. To enable participation from all sectors, limited scholarship assistance is available. Please note below your need for tuition assistance, if any.

_____ I do not need scholarship assistance.   _____ I need scholarship assistance in the amount of $_____.

Please send tuition bill to:	_____ Applicant	_____ Applicant's Employer

Send application to:
LEADERSHIP HARNETT
Post Office Box 507
Lillington, NC 27546
(910) 893-7540/(910) 893-5577 Fax
mwillis@harnett.org

Application Deadline:

January 29, 2016

REVISED 12/2015

Exhibit 7.4   Application Form for the Monroe County (Indiana) Citizens' Academy

PURDUE UNIVERSITY

PURDUE EXTENSION

PURDUE EXTENSION | LOCAL FACES Countless Connections

Monroe County
Citizens' Academy
2016

February 8 - April 4
Mondays, 6:00 pm - 9:00 pm

Application for Citizens' Academy
Application Deadline: February 1, 2016

Name: _____

Address: _____

_____

Email: _____

Phone: (H)_____ (C)_____

Why are you interested in Citizens' Academy?

_____
_____
_____
_____
_____

Please mail or bring this form to:

Purdue Extension - Monroe County
3400 South Walnut Street
Bloomington, IN 47401

Participants will receive additional information prior to the program.

For more information, please contact
Purdue Extension - Monroe County Office at
812-349-2575 or monroeces@purdue.edu.

Why Participate?

Community Benefits
- Better informed citizens
- Civically engaged leaders

Personal Benefits
- Learn the services the county offices provide
- Meet county government leaders
- Learn how you can take a more active role in government

Government of Monroe County, Indiana

A former participant said: I've always thought that I was a "good citizen", because I paid taxes, voted and followed the political news. Now I realize that's not enough. A "good citizen" must be an "informed citizen". I was blown away by what I learned in this class! I was truly impressed with the caliber of the county officials - they all were sincere, intelligent and cared deeply about helping the public.

PURDUE AGRICULTURE

Purdue University is an Affirmative Action institution.
If you have special needs, please indicate on the registration form, or call us prior to the meeting at 812-349-2575.

Purdue Extension-Monroe County   https://extension.purdue.edu/monroe/

Exhibit 7.4   Application Form for the Monroe County (Indiana) Citizens' Academy (*continued*)

What is the Citizens' Academy?

The Monroe County Citizens' Academy provides Monroe County residents with an in-depth look at the functions of county government and will educate residents on the "behind the scenes" activities of local government.

. . . .

The **Monroe County Citizens' Academy** will meet **each Monday**, beginning **February 8 and** concluding **April 4** Classes will be held in the evening from **6:00 pm- 9:00 pm**. Classes will meet at various **County Offices**

If you are a resident of Monroe County and you want to learn more about how your county government operates and how you can be more involved, we encourage you to register to participate in this program.

The Monroe County Citizens' Academy is hosted by the Purdue Extension - Monroe County Office, in cooperation with the Monroe County Commissioners and the Monroe County Council.

Meet the County

The Monroe County Citizens' Academy allows its participants to get a behind-the-scenes look at county government. Participants interact with department heads and elected official to learn more about their roles throughout the county.

Participants should be at least eighteen years of age or older. Attendance and commitment is respectfully asked, since you will receive valuable information not only in discussion but also in written form.

There is no cost to participate, however registration is requested.

A complete program agenda will be given to all participants at the first session.

The sessions will take place at the various County Offices which will noted on the program agenda.

The Citizens' Academy is funded and supported by the Monroe County Commissioners and the Monroe County Council.

Conclusion. The Story of Decatur 101

> *Wonderful program—I know a lot more about Decatur now—I love it even more! Thank you for the time, energy, and commitment you have for this class. I have already told 10 people about it.*
>
> Decatur 101 Participant

We want to end with a profile of a successful citizens academy. Linda Harris, coordinator of Decatur (Georgia) 101, shared the program's story in an interview conducted in May 2016. We share it here to illustrate the added value represented by citizens academies and to demonstrate that a successful program need not be huge in terms of budget or time commitment. Indeed, Decatur's program is one of the shortest in terms of program hours, but demand is very high and alumni tend to show up en masse whenever community leaders seek to engage its citizens.

Decatur 101 started out like many other citizens academy programs, as a vision of what could be. Linda Harris, Decatur's assistant director of community and economic development, along with one of her colleagues, envisioned a program that could both inform and involve citizens in the inner workings of their city (an in-town suburb of Atlanta). They had a vision of proactively reaching out to the community in a way that would "create informed and involved citizens."

Leading up to the launch of the first citizens academy in 2000, Harris worked to develop buy-in from other colleagues and community leaders. It was a learning process. "We had to beg people to come that first year." Part of the problem was discovering that Decatur 101 was offered at the same time as the public safety academy. The program was moved to the spring, and over time, the number of applications took off. The program offered one session annually for the first several years, but then increased demand made it possible to expand to two sessions (one during the day, one in the evening) every year. And after more than a decade of offering two sessions per year, the program still maintains a waiting list of up to 20 people each year.

Decatur 101 is somewhat an outlier in that it is one of the shorter programs of its kind. While most citizens academies consist of 8 to 10, 2- to 3-hour sessions, Decatur 101 has 5, 2-hour sessions. A good deal of effort is expended to make each interactive and collaborative. "We wanted to make it interactive and fun, and not just talking heads," says Harris. Each class has an interactive component, such as the scavenger hunt assigned at the beginning of each program that encourages participants to visit areas of the city they may never have been to before. This activity not only helps familiarize participants with the public buildings and spaces around the city, but it also offers them a shared experience they can call upon in bonding with one another on day one. (See Chapter 4.)

Harris strives to get diverse groups of people to apply by offering alternative class times. In 2005, Decatur 101 started offering morning sessions in addition to the regular evening options and began to notice more of a difference in ages among the people who applied. Participants now have the option of going to either the morning or evening session, depending on which time works best with their schedules. Since 2013, the program has started capturing the demographics of its participants in order to better track their impact and to reach out to various demographic groups within the community.

> *This experience was just wonderful. I really didn't know what to expect. As a new resident, I now feel that I know so much more about my "new home" than before. There was so much useful information presented. Thank you so much!*
>
> Decatur 101 Participant

Every lesson and activity people participate in with Decatur 101 is based on the premise that "in the absence of information people will make up their own." One of the main reasons for making the sessions interactive and fun is not only to facilitate the learning process but, also, to help "put a face on government" and establish better rapport between government and citizens. One of the most helpful takeaways graduates receive (according to feedback they provide) is a sheet of paper listing every government official and staff member they came across during the program, including names, titles, short bios, and headshots. Many use this resource as a visual aid when they are out and about in the community as well as when the program holds alumni social events that staff and elected officials will be attending. "People know who we are," says Harris. "Even if we disagree, it's a forum for them to be like, why aren't we doing it this way? . . . Kind of including them in the process."

Decatur 101 has become an important stepping stone for graduates who wish to become, or remain, active members of the community. The application process for the city's volunteer boards and commissions even inquires if the applicant is a graduate of the program. But whether participants become interested in formal local government service or not, Harris is very conscientious about keeping them engaged after graduating from the program. All alumni are added to a mailing list through which they receive timely information about what is going on in the city. Harris also created the Encore program in response to feedback from graduates saying they were interested in knowing about additional opportunities to reconnect and to go more in-depth about important issues in the community. One such session, called "Talking across Differences," engaged alumni in a dialogue about collaboration among community members with differing perspectives. Harris says, "I always ask myself, would I want to go to this? I don't want to have a meeting just to have a meeting."

Harris believes that one of the greatest benefits of Decatur 101 is the trust it builds between participants and their city government and also among the participants themselves. She notes that participants almost universally walk away with a sense that the city is "not big, bad government . . . [they] are real people [we] can see or call." Participants know that city staff are approachable and that they are willing to engage citizens in discussions around complex issues they care about.

It is because of that trust and sense of community that Decatur 101 alumni tend to show up in force whenever the city formally engages its residents. For a strategic planning meeting held in 2010, 800 people attended, and Harris estimated that 70 percent of them were Decatur 101 alumni.

Moving forward, Harris is exploring the idea of instituting an online component of the citizens academy she helped launch more than 15 years ago but is in the process of figuring out how to do so without losing the relationship building aspect that makes Decatur 101 so appealing. With the current format, these passionate, dedicated community members come out of graduation with an expanded community network that includes residents they would not know otherwise as well as local government staff. This key benefit is a primary reason why many graduates recommend to their acquaintances that they apply to a future session

> *Great job. Wonderful to meet everyone involved in running our city. I feel like I have a more personal connection now.*
>
> Decatur 101 Participant

> *Fabulous! Thank you! I want to get more involved!*
>
> Decatur 101 Participant

Decatur 101 participants show off their graduation certificates and swag

and why they return for Encore or other reunion event. According to Harris, not having that face-to-face interactive component "sort of cuts against what we see as the biggest piece of this, which is people connecting with each other." However, as demonstrated by the evolution of Encore, the city is always open to growing and expanding based on feedback provided by its citizens.

Decatur 101 is a great example of a successful citizens academy, but it also has more than 15 years of trial and error under its belt. To those who are thinking about starting a citizens academy, or are currently running a program and looking for ideas to make it even better, we hope the best practices and concepts outlined in this book have been helpful. For even more resources, consider visiting the University of North Carolina (UNC) School of Government (SOG) online resource dedicated to citizens academies at www.sog.unc.edu/resources/microsites/citizens-academies.

About the Authors

Ricardo S. Morse is an associate professor of public administration at the University of North Carolina School of Government. His research, teaching, and consulting focus on public leadership, collaborative governance, and civic engagement. He has published numerous articles and book chapters and is the lead editor of two books, *Transforming Public Leadership for the 21st Century* (2007) and *Innovations in Public Leadership Development* (2008). He co-founded and co-coordinates the Community Engagement Learning Exchange (http://cele.sog.unc.edu), a School of Government blog dedicated to exchanging experiences and insights on community engagement among practitioners, local citizens, and scholars. Rick holds bachelor and master's degrees in public policy from Brigham Young University and a doctorate in public administration/public affairs from Virginia Tech.

Sabrina M. Willard is a Class of 2017 candidate in the Master of Public Administration program at the University of North Carolina School of Government. She is also a candidate in the Community Preparedness and Disaster Management graduate certificate program at the University of North Carolina at Chapel Hill Gillings School of Public Health. Her professional experience includes internship positions at various levels of government, including the Orange County, North Carolina, Health Department, the Arizona State Senate, and the U.S. Government Accountability Office.

Michelle Y. Holder serves as a management analyst and citizens academy coordinator in Aspen, Colorado. She was first introduced to citizen academies as a participant in Gainesville 101, a program conducted in her college town, and the experience sparked a passion to pursue further studies and practice in local government management and community engagement. Michelle is a 2015 graduate of the Master of Public Administration program at the University of North Carolina School of Government.

Index

Montgomery County–Christiansburg (Va.) Citizens Academy, 28, 73, 140–42, 143
Moore County (N.C.) Government 101, 57, 58, 59
multi-government programs, 139–42
mutual or collaborative learning, 77–78, 88–91

N
National Association of Counties (NACo), 23
National Conference on Citizenship, 5
National League of Cities (NLC), 1–2, 4, 5–6, 7, 23, 46
need for program, evaluating, 120, 121
neighborhood colleges. *See* citizens academies
NLC. *See* National League of Cities
non-profits, partnering with, 145–51
number of participants per class, 50
number of sessions, 28

N
Oakland (Calif.) Citizens' Academy, 47, 54, 55
Ocean City (Md.) University, 52, 64–65, 110–11, 125, 129
organizational learning, 118–20

O
PACT. *See* Redwood City (Calif.) Partnership Academy for Community Teamwork
participants, 45–72. *See also* inclusiveness and diversity
    adjusting schedules and programs for, 26, 28–30
    advertising to and recruitment of, 54–57, 64–65, 68
    alternative language programs for, 54
    applications, 59–61, 66–67, 69–72
    demographics, 26, 28–30, 50, 52–54
    elected officials and staff as, 52
    evaluation surveys, 120–25
    minimum age of, 50
    number per class, 50
    questions to consider, 62–63
    residency requirements for, 50, 52
    selecting, 57–59
    targeted participation model, 52–54
    teenagers as, 51, 59, 60
    waiting lists, 59